WHO MURDERED
YITZHAK RABIN?

Updated English Edition

Barry Chamish

D1616263

BROOKLINE BOOKS • CAMBRIDGE, MA

Library of Congress Cataloging-in-Publication Data
Chamish, Barry, 1952-
    Who murdered Yitzhak Rabin?
    p. cm.
    ISBN 1-57129-080-8
        1. Rabin, Yitzhak, 1922- 2. °'mir, Yig®'1. 3. Political violence--Israel.
        4. Right-wing extremists--Israel 5. Orthodox Judaism--Political Aspects--Israel
        6. Assassination--Religious aspects--Judaism 7. Israel--Politics and government.
        I. Title.

DS126.6.R32 C45 2000
364.15'24'09569409049--dc21   00-023582
                                                                        CIP

cover illustration and design by Nathan Budoff
Printed in The United States of America by Banta Book Group

Further material by Barry Chamish regarding Rabin's murder may be accessed at the follow-ing website:
www.webseers.com/rabin

Published by
BROOKLINE BOOKS, INC.
P.O. Box 381047
Cambridge, Massachusetts 02238-1047
Order toll-free: 1-800-666-BOOK

Yitzhak Rabin was murdered
on November 4, 1995.

CONTENTS

PHOTOS

ACKNOWLEDGMENTS

There are many people in Israel, who want the truth of the Rabin assassination smothered and fewer, who want it exposed. The latter have endured much public and professional wrath for their courage, and I thank them all for their inner strength.

My choice of an inexperienced researcher, Yechiel Mann, was entirely rewarded by his discoveries. As usual, Joel Bainerman provided inspired perspective. Natan Gefen and Marc Weiss provided solid investigatory proofs. Brian Bunn organized a famous lecture that exposed my work to a national audience. I am forever grateful for his courage, as I am to all, who invited me to address their organizations. Journalists Avi Segal, Emma Sodnikov, and Zeev Barcella are the bravest and the best; they were the first in Israel to conclude I might be right and wrote so in lengthy articles. I am forever grateful to Evgenia Kravchick for skillfully translating my work for a widespread Russian-language readership. Jay Bushinsky and his partner Linda Amar of NBC-Extra were the first correspondents from a popular foreign media, who understood the strength of my case and had the integrity to let America know. Eli Wohlgelernter is to be commended for his balanced front page report in the usually timid *Jerusalem Post*. Professor Arieh Zaretski is the person I credit most for having my work accepted by so many in academia.

By the end of 1997, numerous Israeli journalists finally stuck their necks out and, risking the mockery of their peers, examined the facts objectively. They include: Professor Hillel Weiss, Adir Zik, Dr. Joel Cohen, Gadi Blum, Shimon Zilber, Hagai Huberman, Baruch Gordon, Hagai Segal, Ram Ezrach, and Melech Klosner. The previous journalists are mostly religious or politically conservative. Yuval Yoaz deserves special mention because he gave me a fair shake in *Anashim*, a magazine, which appeals to the constituency in Israel, which does not want to believe these events could have happened.

Finally, there are about fifty people, who provided me with essential information but would not want to be acknowledged by name. You know who you are. You know how much your information meant to the contents of this book.

INTRODUCTION—
A SLOPPY CONSPIRACY

There are successful assassinations where the murderers never get caught. The conspiracy to murder Yitzhak Rabin shouldn't be one of them. It was a sloppy conspiracy and the murderers could eventually be brought to justice. But, for a variety of reasons, the Israeli political establishment is ignoring many indisputable clues to avoid pursuing justice.

Yitzhak Rabin was an ideal target for assassination. As Prime Minister, a peace process with the PLO and Syria was forced upon him from abroad. He became a willing advocate of a diplomacy, which was leading to Israel's sure demise. He faced mortal danger from two opposing camps: the minions of Israelis who fought the peace process and the foreign and Israeli powerbrokers who supported it. The former was blamed for the murder while the latter was responsible for it.

This book does not, however, delve into Rabin's murky diplomatic ties, nor does it name who gave the order for the assassination. No one knows who was at the top of the conspiracy. But the reader will discover who had to have been involved at the operational level, and learn just as surely that Rabin could not have possibly been killed by his accused murderer, Yigal Amir.

To keep the peace process on track, it was vital that all opponents be discredited. Opposition came from all quarters in Israel, even from within Rabin's Labor Party (one faction of which eventually broke off to join the later Likud-led government). Typical of the most vocal opponents, Yigal Amir was religious, right-wing, and Sephardi. He was the most politically useful patsy that could be devised.

Yigal Amir was an activist of the supposed anti-peace process organization, Eyal (acronym for the Organization of Jewish Warriors). Eyal, however, was a front created by the General Security Services (Shabak, Israel's FBI). Helmed by Avishai Raviv, a Shabak agent since 1987, Eyal was created as part of a covert operation designed to attract anti-peace process radicals and set them up for arrest. Ample testimony has been gathered from people who witnessed Raviv's methods. Herein it will be made clear that one of his duties was to provoke Yigal Amir into shooting Rabin.

Many, if not most of the Shabak agents, and possibly several policemen on duty the night of the assassination, were instructed to allow a sting operation to take place. Yigal Amir would be provided with a gun loaded with blanks. He would shoot at Rabin and be caught red-handed. Rabin's government would then have the justification to order a nationwide crackdown on opponents of the peace process.

And indeed, after Rabin was shot, Shabak agents yelled, "They're blanks," "It was a toy gun," "It's an exercise," "They were caps," "It wasn't real," "Dummy bullets," and the like because they thought the sting had taken place.

But there was a double-cross. Amir shot his blank bullets and Rabin, very much alive, was shoved into his limousine, where the real assassin lay in wait. What should have been a one-minute trip to the hospital took over eight minutes meandering down the dark streets of Tel Aviv. During that time, the murderer completed his job and left the car.

This is neither speculation nor theory. The author has collected hundreds of pages of police reports, court protocols, and public and personal testimony—enough to demonstrate the veracity of these conclusions.

Just a few of the clues the conspirators left behind include:

- The amateur film of the assassination showing the back door of Rabin's "empty" limousine being slammed shut before he enters the vehicle.

- The same film documenting that Rabin's bodyguards allowed Amir to take a clear shot at the Prime Minister and that Rabin survived it.

- Testimony from witnesses a few feet from Rabin, including his wife, who saw him continue walking briskly after being "shot." Ten minutes after the "shooting," one witness, Miriam Oren, told a national television audience, "Rabin wasn't hurt. I saw him walk into the car."

- Testimony from numerous security and police officers, who did not believe Rabin was shot because he didn't fall, cry out in pain, or bleed.

- Police laboratory tests concluding that Rabin was shot point blank, though the government's commission of inquiry concluded that Amir shot from a good half meter's distance.

Who Murdered Yitzhak Rabin?

- The Police Ballistics report stating that Amir's clip contained only eight bullets, though he loaded nine.

- The unexplainable disappearance of the bullets for eleven hours after their supposed removal from Rabin's body.

- The death certificate—signed by Dr. Mordecai Gutman, one of the surgeons who operated on Rabin—stating that Rabin was shot through the chest from the front and that his spine was shattered, claims backed the same evening by an operating room nurse, the Health Minister, the Director of Ichilov Hospital, a patient, and even then Foreign Minister Shimon Peres. The official version of events has Amir shooting Rabin in the back with no spinal damage.

The conspiracy was so bungled that not only was abundant physical evidence left behind, but the conspirators themselves didn't coordinate their testimony with one another, and ended up contradicting each other at every opportunity.

It would have been so simple if an aggrieved radical had actually assassinated Rabin. But Amir's deep ties to the very people who were charged with protecting the Prime Minister begins to demonstrate the web of deceit and criminality perpetrated by the Shabak.

Amir and Rabin were not the only victims. There were many others, both Jew and Arab. We can only hope that this book will help see that they were the last.

1
אֲ

THE CONSPIRACY
EMERGES—QUICKLY

It took almost two years for the American public to suspect a conspiracy was involved in the Kennedy assassination. It took less than two weeks before suspicions arose among many Israelis that Yitzhak Rabin was not murdered by a lone gunman.

The first to propose the possibility, on November 11, 1995, was Professor Michael Harseger, a Tel Aviv University historian. He told the Israeli press, "There is no rational explanation for the Rabin assassination. There is no explaining the breakdown. In my opinion there was a conspiracy involving the Shabak. It turns out the murderer was in the Shabak when he went to Riga. He was given documents that permitted him to buy a gun. He was still connected to the Shabak at the time of the murder."

Harseger's instincts were correct, but he believed the conspirators were from a right-wing rogue group in the Shabak. It wasn't long before suspicions switched to the left. On the 16th of November, a territorial leader (and later Knesset Member), Benny Elon, called a press conference during which he announced, "There is a strong suspicion that Eyal and Avishai Raviv not only were connected loosely to the Shabak but worked directly for the Shabak. This group incited the murder. I insist that not only did the Shabak know about Eyal, it founded and funded the group."

The public reaction was basically, "Utter nonsense." Yet Elon turned out to be right on the money. How did he know ahead of everyone else?

Film director, Merav Ktorza, and her cameraman, Alon Eilat, interviewed Elon in January 1996. Off camera he told them, "Yitzhak Shamir called me into his office a month before the assassination and told me, 'They're planning to do another Arlosorov on us. Last time they did it, we didn't get into power for fifty years. I want you to identify anyone you hear of threatening to murder Rabin and stop him.'"

In 1933, left wing leader, Chaim Arlosorov, was murdered in Tel Aviv and the right wing Revisionists were blamed for it. This was Israel's first political murder and its repercussions were far stronger than those of the Rabin assassination, which saw the new Likud Revisionists assume power within a year.

Shamir was the former head of the Mossad's European desk and had extensive intelligence ties. He was informed of the impending assassination in October. Two witnesses heard Elon make this remarkable claim, but he would not go on camera with it or make any other statement. Shortly after his famous press conference and testimony to the Shamgar Commission, Elon stopped talking publicly about the assassination.

There are two theories about his sudden shyness. Shmuel Cytryn, the Hebron resident who was jailed without charge for first identifying Raviv as a Shabak agent, has hinted that Elon played some role in the Raviv affair and he was covering his tracks at the press conference.

Ktorza and Eilat believe that pressure was applied on Elon using legal threats against his niece Margalit Har Shefi. Because of her acquaintance with Amir, she was charged as an accessory to the assassination. To back up their threats, the Shabak had Amir write a rambling, incriminating letter to her from prison. The fear of his niece spending a decade in jail would surely have been enough to put a clamp down on Elon.

Utter nonsense turned into utter reality the next night when journalist, Amnon Abramovitch, announced on national television that the leader of Eyal, Yigal Amir's good friend, Avishai Raviv, was a Shabak agent codenamed "Champagne" for the bubbles of incitement he raised.

The announcement caused a national uproar. One example from the media reaction sums up the shock. *Maariv* wrote:

> "Amnon Abramovitch dropped a bombshell last night, announcing that Avishai Raviv was a Shabak agent codenamed 'Champagne.' Now we ask the question, why didn't he report Yigal Amir's plan to murder Rabin to his superiors...? In conversations with security officials, the following picture emerged. Eyal was under close supervision of the Shabak. They supported it monetarily for the past two years. The Shabak knew the names of all Eyal members, including Yigal Amir."

That same day, 11/19/95, *Yediot Ahronot* reported details of a conspiracy that will not go away.

> "There is a version of the Rabin assassination that includes a deep conspiracy within the Shabak. The Raviv affair is a cornerstone of the conspiracy plan.
> "Yesterday, a story spread among the settlers that Amir was supposed to fire a blank bullet, but he knew he was being set up so he replaced the

blanks with real bullets. The story explains why after the shooting, the bodyguards shouted that 'the bullets were blanks.' The story sounds fantastic but the Shabak's silence is fueling it."

Without the 'Champagne' leak, this book would likely not have been written. Despite all the conflicting testimony at the Shamgar Commission, the book would have been closed on Yigal Amir and the conspiracy would have been a success. But Abramovitch's scoop established a direct sinister connection between the murderer and the people protecting the prime minister.

So who was responsible for the leak? There are two candidates who were deeply involved in the protection of Eyal but probably knew nothing of the plans to murder Rabin. They are then-Police Minister, Moshe Shahal, and then-Attorney General, Michael Ben Yair.

Shahal was asked for his reaction to the Abramovitch annoucement. He said simply, "Amnon Abramovitch is a very reliable journalist." In short, he immediately verified the Champagne story. Not that he didn't know the truth, as revealed in the Israeli press:

Maariv, 11/24/95
"The police issued numerous warrants against Avishai Raviv but he was never arrested. There was never a search of his home."

Kol Ha Ir, 1/96
Nati Levy: "It occurs to me in retrospect that I was arrested on numerous occasions but Raviv, not once. There was a youth from Shiloh who was arrested for burning a car. He told the police that he did it on Raviv's orders. Raviv was held and released the same day."

Yediot Ahronot 12/5/95:
"When they aren't involved in swearing-in ceremonies, Eyal members relax in a Kiryat Arba apartment near the home of Baruch Goldstein's family. The police have been unsuccessfully searching for the apartment for some time."

Everyone in the media knew about the apartment, as did everyone in Kiryat Arba in Hebron. It was in the same building as the apartment of Baruch Goldstein, the alleged murderer of twenty-nine Arabs in the Hebron massacre of March 1994. The police left it alone because Raviv used it for surveillance.

Raviv was also immune to arrest for such minor crimes as arson and threatening to kill Jews and Arabs in televised swearing-in ceremonies. But police inaction was inexcusable in two well-publicized incidents.

Yerushalayim, 11/10/95
"Eyal activists have been meeting with Hamas and Islamic Jihad members
to plan joint operations."

This item was reported throughout the country, but Avishai Raviv was
not arrested for treason, terrorism and cavorting with the enemy. Less ex-
plainable yet, was the police reaction to Raviv taking responsibility—credit,
as he called it—for the murder of three Palestinians in a town near Hebron.

On December 11, 1993, three Arabs were killed by men wearing Israeli
army uniforms. Eyal called the media the next day claiming the slaughter was
its work. But Moshe Shahal did not order the arrest of Eyal members. Rather,
according to *Globes* 12/13/93, "Shahal told the cabinet that heightened action was being taken to find the killers and to withdraw the legal rights of the
guilty organization."

Supposedly Shahal knew that Eyal was behind the murder. In fact, he
knew that Eyal was not responsible, he knew they took responsibility to blacken
the name of West Bank settlers and he said nothing. After a week of international condemnation of the settlers, the army arrested the real murderers, four
Arabs from the town.

At that point Shahal should have had Raviv arrested for issuing the false
proclamation on behalf of Eyal. But Shahal did not because he was ordered
not to interfere with this Shabak operation.

As was Attorney-General, Michael Ben Yair, who was so terrified of what
could be revealed at the Shamgar Commission that he sat in on every session
on behalf of the government. He later approved, along with Prime Minister
Peres, the sections to be hidden from the public.

After the assassination, it emerged that two left wing Knesset (Parliament) members had previously submitted complaints against Eyal to Ben
Yair. On March 5, 1995, Dedi Tzuker asked Ben Yair to investigate Eyal after
it distributed inciteful literature at a Jerusalem high school. And on September 24, 1995, Yael Dayan requested that Ben Yair open an investigation of
Eyal in the wake of its televised vow to spill the blood of Jews and Arabs who
stood in the way of their goals. He ignored both petitions, later explaining,
"Those requests should have been submitted to the army or the Defense Minister," who happened to be Yitzhak Rabin.

Both Shahal and Ben Yair were, probably unwittingly, ordered to cover up
Eyal's incitements. But when one incitement turned out to be the murder of
Rabin, one of them panicked and decided to place all the blame on the Shabak.
Which one?

According to Abramovitch, "I have a legal background, so my source was a high ranking legal official." It sounds like the winner is Ben Yair...which hardly exonerates him or Shahal for supplying Eyal with immunity from arrest or prosecution, without which, the assassination of Yitzhak Rabin would not have been possible.

However, Ben Yair opened a police complaint against the 'leak', and as late as June of 1996, reporter Abramovich was summoned to give evidence.

The leak, thus may have come from a "traitor" in Ben Yair or Shahal's offices. And because there are Israelis who know the truth and are willing to secretly part with it, this book could be written.

2

ב

PROVOKING AMIR
INTO MURDER

Numerous witnesses saw Avishai Raviv provoke Yigal Amir into assassinating Yitzhak Rabin. Raviv utilized a long campaign of psychological pressure on Amir and Amir alone. He did not concentrate his efforts on any other Eyal activist. Amir was chosen for the task and for good reason. Not many people are capable of murder even if prodded relentlessly into it. Somehow Raviv knew Amir was the only fit candidate for the job.

Yigal Amir spent the spring and summer of 1992 in Riga, Latvia on assignment from the Liaison Department of the Prime Minister's Office, usually called Nativ. In one of the greater ironies of the assassination drama, it was Prime Minister Rabin who was ultimately responsible for assigning Amir to the Riga post. Or to put it another way, Amir was an employee of the man he was blamed for murdering.

Yet there was an even greater irony. Acting on reports from the State Comptroller of massive financial corruption, Rabin was preparing to shut down Nativ. Some have considered this a motive for the murder. An early, and false, excuse of the Shabak to explain how Amir was let into the sterile area was that he presented government credentials in the form of his Nativ identity card.

Nativ was and is a nest of spies. Founded in the early 1950s as a liaison between Israel and Jews trapped behind the Iron Curtain, over the years, according to *Haaretz* (11/95), "It had developed its own independent intelligence and operational agenda."

A hint of what that means was revealed in June 1996 when the Russian government arrested, and then expelled, a Nativ worker named Daniel for illegally acquiring classified satellite photos. Indignant, the Russians threatened to close all of Israel's immigration offices in the country. The indignation was renewed in January 1997 when Daniel was appointed Nativ's head of intelligence.

Another source of indignation is the fact that Nativ has been granting visas to Israel for major criminals including members of the Russian mafia and a former president of the Ukraine who escaped to Tel Aviv with $60 million stolen from his country's treasury. The escape occurred barely five months after a meeting with Police Minister, Moshe Shahal, and Foreign Minister, Shimon Peres, in Kiev.

Within days of the assassination, the government went on full tilt to explain away Amir's Riga sojourn. First, the government admitted that Amir was a Hebrew teacher there for five months. But since he had no teacher's degree, nor spoke Latvian, the story didn't wash. So Police Minister, Moshe Shahal, explained that Amir was a security guard there for only three months.

That explanation had its drawbacks, as elaborated by Alex Fishman in *Yediot Ahronot*, who wrote, "As a guard he was trained by the Shabak in techniques and weaponry, training he used to deadly effect on that miserable Saturday night in Tel Aviv."

The government clearly didn't like Amir's Shabak ties speculated upon, so Aliza Goren, the spokeswoman for the Prime Minister's Office told reporters, "Amir was never in Riga and anyone who reports that he was is being totally irresponsible."

That ploy fell to bits when the BBC's *Panorama* program interviewed Amir's family and filmed his passport. Stamped within was a bold CCCP. Goren had lied and by implication was guilty of covering up a fact the government clearly didn't want known.

Speculation was rife by the beginning of 1996 that Amir was on an intelligence mission on behalf of the Prime Minister's Office in Riga. So Israel Television's Channel One broadcast a long interview with Moshe Levanon, the former head of Nativ. He insisted that his organization had no intelligence ties and then presented a series of photos illustrating his work. Included was one of him standing with former CIA Director George Bush, apparently in Russia.

Amir was in Riga for a reason, and the mild-mannered soldier returned in the fall of 1992 with a changed personality. He was now Amir, the campus radical of Bar Ilan University. Something happened in Riga to alter his mindset. But whatever it was, Amir was still not quite capable of murder. Avishai Raviv had his job cut out to exploit Amir's psychological weaknesses and transform him into a political assassin.

Maariv, 9/11/96

"'It was said amongst us that Rabin was a persecutor and could be sentenced to die according to biblical precepts,' related Avishai Raviv at his hearing yesterday."

Maariv, 10/11/95
"An Eyal poster on Bar Ilan campus showed a photo of Rabin covered in blood. Interested students were asked to phone Raviv's beeper number for more information."

Maariv, 12/12/95
"Several times I heard from Yigal Amir that he intended to hurt the prime minister, but I didn't take it seriously," Avishai Raviv testified to the Shamgar Commission."

Behind closed doors, Raviv testified that he once had a discussion with Amir about bullets for the gun. One implication of this testimony is that Raviv may have supplied Amir with what he thought were blank bullets.

Maariv, 24/11/95
"According to Sarah Eliash, a schoolteacher working at the Shomron Girls Seminary, some of her pupils heard Raviv encourage Amir to murder Rabin. Raviv told Amir, 'Show us you're a man. Do it.'"

Yediot Ahronot, 11/12/95
"One of the pupils said Raviv called a few government members 'monsters,' and added that it was necessary to blow up the whole government to get rid of the 'persecutors.'"

Another pupil told how Raviv used quotes from biblical commentary to prove the need to kill Rabin.

Uri Dan and Dennis Eisenberg, writing for the *Jerusalem Post,* elaborated on the girls' later testimony behind closed doors at the Shamgar Commission:

"Sarah Eliash had already appeared voluntarily before the commission and related how her pupils had run to see her on the night of the killing. In tears they said they knew Yigal Amir. They had met both Amir and Avishai Raviv, the General Security Services (GSS) agent, at the settlement of Barkan last summer. 'We used to see Raviv and Amir on Saturdays during last summer,' they related.

"These gatherings were arranged by Yigal...Raviv was real macho. He kept saying to Yigal: "You keep talking about killing Rabin. Why don't you do it? Are you frightened? You say you want to do it. Show us that you're a man. Show us what you're made of.""

The other girls present corroborated the evidence. How did Amir react to the goading by Raviv? All replied in roughly the same way:

"He didn't react. He just sat there and said nothing or changed the subject."

Geula Amir, Yigal's mother, "writes" in the February 1997 *George Magazine* (her piece was actually ghost-written by two Jerusalem-based journalists):

"According to Yigal's friends and others who have since testified in court, Raviv seemed to be obsessed with one topic: killing Rabin. He and Yigal frequently engaged in discussions about the feasibility of the assassination... Several young women said that they recognized Yigal and Raviv from a Sabbath retreat. The girls told their teacher, Sarah Eliash, that Raviv had denounced several Rabin government officials as "traitors." During several marathon ideological discussions that weekend, Raviv had attempted to goad Yigal into killing Rabin, ridiculing his cowardice for not being willing to kill a 'traitor.'"

Eran Agelbo, testifying as a witness for the defense at Yigal's trial, revealed that Raviv had said that Rabin was a 'Rodef'—the Hebrew term for someone who endangers others and therefore should be killed. Agelbo also maintained that Raviv had verbally pressured Yigal to attempt an assassination of Rabin.

"Raviv told Yigal and others that there was a judgment on Yitzhak Rabin. He said, 'Rabin should die and whoever killed him was a righteous person.' Raviv had a powerful influence on Yigal. He continuously emphasized to him and other students that whoever implemented the judgment against Rabin was carrying out a holy mission."

Nice talk from a Shabak agent—and so much for Raviv and other Shabak officers' claims that Amir came up with the idea to kill Rabin all by himself. To acquire original testimony I phoned one of Sarah Eliash's pupils. She began talking to me in Hebrew, but the phone was taken from her by her American-born father. A twenty-minute discussion took place, extracts of which follow:

"___ is not willing to talk to you, do you understand? She has nothing to say."

"We'll never get to the truth if she doesn't."

"Find someone else if you can. I'm not willing to let anything happen to my daughter. You have to understand that, don't you? You don't know what's going on. They promised her if she testified that nothing would happen afterward; no arrests or threats. They lied. She can't talk to you and that's that."

"What about her civil duty? What kind of a country will it be if everyone lets criminals off?"

"I used to think like that. This is no democracy. You don't know what it is. When I came here I thought it was to be free as a Jew. Now I just want to avoid getting in trouble. I can't tell you what they said they'd do to her if she talked anymore."

In total, over a dozen people testified to seeing Raviv prod Amir into killing Rabin. But that was not the sum total of his involvement. There was another function to be taken care of after Amir "shot" Rabin. Arieh Oranj told me,

> "Our plan was to go to Gaza to participate in another demonstration to counterbalance the one in Tel Aviv. But at the last minute he changed his mind and led us to the Tel Aviv rally. Not two minutes after the shooting, Raviv told us, 'Do you know who did it? Yigal Amir.'"

Maariv, 11/10/95
> "Last Saturday night, minutes after Prime Minister Rabin was shot and well before the killer was identified, Avishai Raviv, head of Eyal, already announced that the assassin was Yigal Amir."

Immediately after the shooting, several reporters received messages on their beepers proclaiming that 'Eyal takes responsibility for the deed.' Minutes after the shooting, an unknown group called Jewish Vengeance called dozens of reporters leaving the message:

> "We missed this time but next time we'll get him."

After Rabin's death was announced, the same group left a followup message for the same reporters, taking responsibility for the murder. Clearly, the message leaver—most likely Raviv—originally thought Amir was supposed to miss Rabin and was caught off guard when it turned out Rabin was assassinated.

Maariv, 11/19/95
> "As recalled, minutes after the assassination, before any reporter even knew Rabin's condition, Avishai Raviv, head of Eyal, passed on the identity of the killer. Thinking that it was a mere assassination attempt, he anonymously passed on his 'We Missed' but we'll get him next time message."

Moments later he told a *Maariv* reporter, "We have no connection to this act. This is not our type of operation." Despite the denial, he gave out details about Yigal Amir including his exact name, that he was a student at Bar Ilan, and his army record.

Dan and Eisenberg interviewing an unnamed Shabak official:

> "If this wasn't a deliberate set-up," we asked, "what is? How do you react to the evidence of the bystanders who heard Raviv talk to someone on his mobile

phone at the peace rally and announce that it was Amir who had shot Rabin— 40 minutes before Amir's identity was released on TV and radio?

"Of course the Shabak official didn't react. He said the testimony was unproven. What else could he say? If the testimony of so many people is true, then Avishai Raviv knew ahead of time that Amir was going to murder Rabin. And unless he kept this fact from his superiors, so did his officers in the unit he worked for, the Jewish Department of the Shabak, who had to have informed their superior, the head of the Shabak, Carmi Gillon.

"If Raviv genuinely withheld his prior knowledge of Amir's intentions, then he is an accessory to murder, if not an actual accomplice. However, no one in the Shabak, police or government is treating him that way. He has not been charged with any crime and has been hidden away in jobs aiding autistic children."

Raviv's activities on the night of the assassination strongly suggest that he thought Amir was not actually going to succeed in killing Rabin. His duty was to accept responsibility for the attempted murder on behalf of Eyal and Jewish Vengeance and thus to link the murderer to a radical, right wing religious organization. Thus, he had no compunctions about bragging to everyone within listening distance that Amir was the shooter, 40 minutes before anyone in the media knew his identity.

But Raviv, like many other Shabak agents, was double-crossed. The supposedly benign and justifiable plan to have Amir caught in the act to promote the peace process had turned into a murder they didn't expect. Obviously caught unaware, Raviv corrected his first telephoned press announcement after Rabin's death became official.

After that, he, like many other Shabak agents, police officers and Rabin associates in the government became part of a murder coverup. They had no choice. They had all willingly conspired to keep "peace" alive by blaming the opposing camp for an assassination attempt. This was a crime that would end careers, smear reputations and land long prison terms. And if that wasn't frightening enough, there was always the knowledge that murderers have no compunction about killing twice.

While one of Eyal's main purposes was to enroll young idealists and radicalize them, another was to eliminate political leaders. Yitzhak Rabin was not the first victim, just the most permanent. Preceding him was future prime minister Binyamin Netanyahu.

One month before Rabin's assassination, on October 5, 1995 another kind of rally took place in Jerusalem. A quarter of a million people gathered to protest the government's "peace" diplomacy. The featured speaker was Binyamin Netanyahu. The sheer size of the protest, which clogged downtown Jerusalem's streets for eight blocks, shocked the supporters of the peace process.

To counterbalance the massive demonstration, two of the supporters—former Likud mayor of Tel Aviv, Shlomo Lahat, and a mysterious Frenchman who had been bankrolling a campaign on behalf of the peace process, Jean Frydman—decided to organize an equally large demonstration in Tel Aviv. Even after busing many thousands of political hacks and youth group members, plus thousands of Israeli Arabs to beef up the attendance, only about half as many people showed up. And it proved to be the setting where the Prime Minister was assassinated.

As was Netanyahu at the Jerusalem rally. Although it was only a character assassination, it served the same purpose of eliminating him from the political arena. And the man behind the assassination was also the same: Shabak officer Avishai Raviv. The weapon he used was a poster of Rabin wearing a Gestapo uniform, which Netanyahu was wrongly accused of having approved. Thus, he was later accused of creating the atmosphere which led directly to Rabin's murder. Ironically, it was Rabin himself who made the accusation in the Knesset that Netanyahu was inciting violence.

The implications are profound. The Prime Minister is responsible for the Shabak and for approving its activities. Unless the Shabak dared to work behind his back, Rabin approved the Raviv operation, thus signing his own death warrant, and in all likelihood he also approved the use of the poster to humiliate Netanyahu.

Avishai Raviv's poster of Rabin portrayed in an SS uniform.

Avishai Raviv holds the weapon suspected in the murder of Rabin. On his t-shirt is a picture of Rabin and the caption: "No Rest for Traitors."

Yediot Ahronot, 11/19/95

"According to testimony from Judea and Samaria Council spokesman, Aharon Domev, Avishai Raviv along with other Eyal people were seen on the night of the demonstration in Zion Square (Jerusalem), October 5, distributing the poster."

Yediot Ahronot, 11/20/95

"Channel One reporter, Nitzan Khen, told viewers of last night's news program that just a few minutes before beginning to broadcast from the demonstration of the right at Zion Square, he was given a leaflet showing Rabin in a Gestapo uniform by Avishai Raviv.

Khen: "Raviv came up to me with two other people known to me, an Eyal activist and a Kach member. They came to the broadcast van and gave me the leaflet. After five or ten minutes Raviv returned to make sure I had broadcast it."

Yediot Ahronot, 11/12/95

Police Captain Yehuda Saidoff: "I concluded that Nitzan Khen has a wild imagination and poor memory for facts. Raviv was more believable to me." Raviv told Saidoff that he received just one copy of the leaflet from a Yeshivah student named Aharon Victor and, when he got home, he ripped it up.

Yediot Ahronot, 27/11/95

"In Jerusalem yesterday, a 16-year-old Yeshivah student was remanded for three days for distributing a leaflet of Yitzhak Rabin in an SS uniform at the rally in Zion Square. He admitted guilt and said he regretted his actions. According to him, Avishai Raviv was responsible for distributing the leaflet."

Maariv, 27/11/95

"The police will question Avishai Raviv on suspicion that he distributed leaflets showing Rabin in an SS uniform at the right wing rally at Zion Square. One of the two arrested Yeshivah students had close ties to Raviv. Police will question other Yeshivah students to establish the extent of the suspects' ties with Raviv."

At the time of the demonstration, when Rabin was very much alive, the issue of who distributed the leaflet was marginal. It didn't matter who distributed it, the issue was that Netanyahu didn't condemn the blown-up poster and leaflets from the podium. But Netanyahu couldn't and didn't see the posters from the stage. When he tried to explain that fact to the Knesset, Rabin indignantly walked out of the chamber.

And at the time, it seemed he had every right to put on his show of anger. But within two weeks of his death, the public knew about Raviv's role in the Shabak and the issue looked quite different. Nitzan Khen testified at the

Shamgar Commission hearings that Raviv and another Eyal member gave
him the leaflet of Rabin in a Gestapo uniform. As Defense Minister, Rabin
was responsible for Shabak activities. He knew exactly who Raviv and Eyal
were. At maximum, he approved the poster operation. At a minimum, he
knew it was a Shabak ploy to weaken opposition to the peace process. Either
way, by walking out of the Knesset while Netanyahu was speaking, he knew
he was playing a dirty trick on his political rival.

How could Rabin have sunk that low? At that point, Netanyahu was
leading Rabin in the polls and a crowd exceeding 200,000 in a city of fewer
than 400,000 Jews had gathered to support him. The country was not divided in two over peace. The vast majority had already soured on the process.
The month before, a *Maariv* poll revealed that 78% of Israelis wanted a
national referendum on whether to carry on the government's peace diplomacy. Members of the government were booed whenever they appeared in
public but none more so than Rabin.

In August, 50,000 fans at a soccer game between Israel and Brazil jeered
in unison when he arrived. Not long after, he was humiliated when his speech
before 1000 English speaking immigrants was marred by the loudest uni-
formly long boo ever heard in Netanya.

A constant vigil of protesters stood outside Rabin's home in suburban Tel
Aviv, but none was so vicious as the Eyal crowd who promised that he and his
wife would hang in a public square like the Mussolinis. Eyal was playing a
sophisticated game of de-legitimizing legal protest through extra-legal extremism.

Raviv and his cohorts could only have gotten away with it with the connivance
of the police, which meant the participation of Police Minister Moshe Shahal, the
same Shahal who was sending mounted policemen into crowds to club thousands
of anti-government demonstrators. Indeed Raviv was held for questioning by the
police for the Rabin/Gestapo officer poster, but as in every previous case where
the police questioned him, he was released shortly after to continue his work.

The public trusted Nitzan Khen and believed him when he testified to
the Shamgar Commission that Avishai Raviv gave him the infamous leaflet.
To cover up the truth, Captain Saidoff took the side of Raviv over the respected journalist Khen. This was just a part of a much more wide-ranging
pattern of a coverup of Eyal's activities by the police and Justice Ministry.

Marc Weiss writes in *The Jewish Press*, 4/25/97:
  "Apparently, the Israeli Justice Department had been informed of Raviv's
  true identity and informant status, and was instructed not to bring agent
  'Champagne' to trial for his illegal actions."

In a document obtained by *The Jewish Press*, the Special Branch of the Israeli Police that deals with extremist groups wrote to Raviv on February 21, 1994 informing him that they were closing their files and declining to prosecute him for the charges of "incitement" against the government. Ironically, the document cites "the lack of public interest" in Raviv's provocations as the reason.

This document—when viewed in light of the fact that it was Raviv's repeated inciting declarations concerning the dire need and biblical permissibility of killing Rabin that laid the very foundation for Yigal Amir's actions—is startling in its implications. Time and again, Raviv was permitted by the State Prosecutor's office to continue on with his campaign of provocation without fear of arrest or prison. The burning question that now cries out for an answer is why.

Why was Raviv never seriously prosecuted, and why didn't Attorney General Michael Ben-Yair order the Shin Bet to immediately curtail its illegal undercover activities? Who was behind these decisions? Moreover, how far up into the Justice Ministry and Prime Minister's Office did the discussions concerning Raviv reach?

Who exactly was behind the decision to give Gillon and Raviv carte blanche to continue to infiltrate and incite? Who permitted Rabin and the Labor Party leadership to utilize the Israeli security services to discredit Netanyahu and the Likud?

Maariv, 11/23/95
"The issue today is the question if Rabin was called to the Shabak head's office after he condemned Netanyahu in the Knesset for the Nazi uniform scandal to be told, 'Mr. Prime Minister, you must know that the people who distributed the leaflet were not our political enemies but our own agents.'"

Yediot Ahronot, 11/24/95
"I can't believe the government itself distributed the leaflet showing the prime minister in a Nazi uniform. I'm certain the Shabak would never have gone ahead with this kind of operation on its own. However, the government exploited the issue viciously to wound the rival political camp, which is made up of half the population.

"It's a scandal. I don't know who decided on the operation that so slandered the prime minister and led to his demise. It's possible that the Shabak agent who distributed the leaflet had something to do with that."

Maariv, 11/20/95
"The editorial staff of *Maariv* asks the police and Justice Ministry...Why haven't you revealed which printing house published the leaflet and why haven't you found the person who ordered the printing?"

Yediot Ahronot, 11/20/95

"Since Rabin's murder, claim Likud spokespeople, their political opposition has waged a cynical campaign aimed at blaming them for the incitement culminating with the poster of Rabin in a Nazi uniform, which led to the murder..."

Benny Begin* asked: "Did the Shabak report to the politicians, before or after the rally, that their agent Raviv distributed the leaflets of the prime minister in a Nazi uniform?"

The difficult question is, did the political establishment know of Raviv's responsibility and cynically exploit it to gain politically by humiliating Binyamin Netanyahu?

Says Binyamin Netanyahu: "If even a part of what is being revealed is true, then there exists a serious threat to our democracy. We demand a full inquiry. We won't permit a coverup."

Immediately after the assassination, the media broadcast numerous claims that Netanyahu killed Rabin by creating the atmosphere which bred the killer. The "proof" of this absurd contention—in fact, Netanyahu was a suspiciously weak opposition leader—was always the poster of Rabin in the SS garb which he allegedly refused to condemn.

In the name of this Shabak-organized pre-assassination incitement, the police were far too ready to initiate a campaign of repression. The Justice Ministry passed a law making a broad definition of incitement illegal, and the roundups began.

Three rabbis accused of declaring Rabin a persecutor were held for questioning, and one was imprisoned without charge for months. An Israeli farmer who expressed satisfaction with the murder during a CNN interview was imprisoned for expressing an inciteful point of view. Shmuel Cytryn of Hebron, who exposed Raviv as a Shabak agent two months before the assassination, was arrested and imprisoned in solitary confinement for four months without ever being charged. Dozens of political opponents were arrested and jailed under Administrative Detention orders which permit arrest without charge. A well prepared clampdown and witchhunt of people opposed to the peace process gripped the nation and all because a poster led to an atmosphere that killed the now besainted former Prime Minister.

---

* Son of Likud founder Menachem Begin. He was originally Netanyahu's Science Minister, but quit over the Hebron withdrawal.

Netanyahu was humiliated time and again for his alleged role in the poster scandal. While Leah Rabin greeted Yasir Arafat in her home during the grieving period, she refused to host Netanyahu or even shake his hand when he offered condolences again at the funeral. Even a year later, when he was prime minister, his attendance at a memorial service for Rabin was marred by protesters accusing him of as good as pulling the trigger by creating the atmosphere of hatred that spawned the murder.

But by now he was well aware of the truth. He knew that a Shabak provocateur was trying to force him out of the political arena by distributing the leaflets and displaying the poster. The May before, during his election campaign, he promised if elected to prosecute Avishai Raviv.

Yet after the assassination, while he was being vilified, he broke his promise to demand a commission of inquiry into Raviv's activities and after the election he broke his promise to prosecute Raviv.

Why wouldn't he want his good name and the good name of his party cleared? Natan Gefen, a diligent researcher of the assassination, thinks he knows why:

> "Before the election, I took the [death] certificate [from Ichilov Hospital, certifying that Rabin was shot through the chest] to two Likud Knesset Members, Yossi Olmert and Dov Shilansky, fully expecting them to consider the political advantages of it. Olmert told me, 'We don't need the document.' A deal was cut, I'm sure of it. Labor didn't bring up Rabin's memory during the campaign and neither did the Likud. Peres stopped campaigning altogether, he threw the television debate with Netanyahu, he was leading in all the polls by 4% the morning of the vote and he still lost. Netanyahu got the full story from sympathizers in the Shabak and he agreed to hush it up in return for winning power. That's why the coverup is still going on like nothing changed after the elections."

Gefen's intuition proved right. Two months later I was invited to a cabinet minister's office. The minister's spokesman informed me that the Likud had prepared a file containing which information about Rabin's murder would be released publicly if Labor utilized Rabin's name in the election campaign.

TELEVISION
SETS UP AMIR

The American political assassination formula sometimes includes creating a believable patsy on television. Lee Harvey Oswald went out of his way to cause a televised stir on a New Orleans street while he was distributing leaflets for Fair Play For Cuba, a committee created by CIA operative, Guy Banister. Gerald Ford's attempted assassin, Squeaky Fromme, was televised constantly as a prominent member of Charles Manson's murder cult. Televising an upcoming assassin serves as later proof that he was an unstable radical and thus provides a motive for murder.

The same tactic was used in Israel. Just as Fair Play For Cuba was a front with one member, Oswald, Eyal—an acronym for The Organization Of Jewish Warriors—was a Shabak straw group with one member, Avishai Raviv. One of Raviv's assignments was to create the most radical anti-peace group of all and to publicize it widely. Originally, the purpose of Eyal was to attract extremists and set them up for arrest. Later, Raviv was ordered to prime Amir for an assassination. It was essential for the assassination plot that Eyal was well known by the public for its extremism, ensuring that Amir's association with it would be motive enough for murder.

To achieve this goal, Raviv needed help from the television media and he got it in the form of Eitan Oren, a documentary director employed by the state-run television station, Channel One.

I assume that Oren was working for the Shabak, but associates of mine in the film industry insist he was just a willing stooge for the station's director-general Moti Kirschenbaum. If so, then Oren had no journalistic ethics whatsoever.

The same charge could be leveled at Moti Kirschenbaum. After being appointed by Rabin, he bankrupted Channel One by eliminating hours of entertainment programming and replacing them with political shows, all heavily pushing the peace process. One example of his slant occurred in March 1994 and was reported widely. Channel One News covered an anti-Rabin rally, much to the prime minister's displeasure. His wife Leah phoned Kirschenbaum and related, "How upset Yitzhak is that the protesters received so much coverage." Kirschenbaum took the hint and initiated a policy change drastically reducing coverage time of legitimate protests.

Instead, his news department sent Oren time and again to cover the most illegitimate protest group of all, the marginal Shabak-front Eyal. I interviewed Eyal "members" Eran Agelbo and Arieh Oranj and instead of the hotheaded extremists I expected, I heard two young kids, terrified of Shabak threats to prosecute them if they went public with what they know about Raviv and Amir.

They described Raviv paying their expenses to appear before Oren's camera and how their every move and statement was stage-directed. To further understand how Channel One and Oren were used to prepare the public for Rabin's assassination, I turn to reports from the Israeli press, collected by Miriam Eilon in one volume called the Champagne File.

Maariv, 11/24/95
"A young Haredi, no more than 18 explained, 'I'm a Yeshiva student and don't have money. Raviv paid all my travel and food expenses. He also promised me more money each time I got Eyal's name mentioned in the media.'"

Hatsofeh, 2/17/95
"Over 500 people attended a memorial service in honor of Baruch Goldstein (who supposedly killed 29 Arabs in Hebron the year before)... Among the organizers was Avishai Raviv, head of Eyal. Many members of the media were also in attendance."

Haaretz, 2/17/95
"Head of Eyal, Avishai Raviv, promised to get even with members of the Judea and Samaria Council who condemned his organization of the Baruch Goldstein memorial service, including Council Secretary, Uri Ariel and Council Spokesman, Aharon Domev. According to Raviv, 'The loss of Goldstein wasn't equal to all the Arabs he killed.'"

Maariv, 17/2/95
"Head of the Kiryat Arba city council, Tzvi Katzover, is threatening to file suit with the Supreme Court to prevent the showing of a television report about Kiryat Arba. In a letter he sent to Communications Minister Shulamit Aloni, Katzover contends that the reporter Eitan Oren staged scenes opposite a poster honoring Baruch Goldstein. 'We don't know what else he staged for his upcoming report,' said Katzover."

In February of the year of Rabin's death, Avishai Raviv organized a memorial service in honor of the mass murderer Baruch Goldstein. The event was condemned by the Jewish territorial leadership. Not that it mattered after Eitan Oren got through with his report. For this report from Hebron, he planted a firm image of irrational Jewish nationalism in the minds of his viewing audience. His news program was broadcast on a Friday night when religious Jews are forbidden to watch television. That way he would elicit the desired response of repulsion from a naive secular population without exposing himself to the wrath and scrutiny of his subjects. To get the effect he wanted, Oren cheated by stage managing at least one extra-radical scene.

In his previous report, Oren stage-managed the whole thing. Raviv dressed up 20 teenagers in tee shirts bearing the name of the right-wing Kach movement, and Oren filmed them in the midst of mock guerrilla warfare.

Haaretz, 5/8/94
"Last Friday night Channel One broadcast a report about a Kach teenage militia training camp whose existence is illegal. Kach symbols and flags were filmed as well as youths wearing Kach tee shirts. Shown also was a patrol in an Arab village and the youths writing inciteful graffiti.

"In light of the report, Police Minister Moshe Shahal had ordered an immediate investigation. The police searched for Avishai Raviv, but he disappeared. He later phoned the police and agreed to show up on Sunday for questioning. Yesterday, he told *Haaretz*, 'We organized the camp to show our solidarity with the people of Hebron and Kiryat Arba. We trained in live weaponry, orienteering, took a hike to Baruch Goldstein's grave and participated in other youth group activities.'"

Raviv admitted that he and his friends initiated the media exposure in order to raise public awareness.

Maariv, 11/24/95
"'We immediately knew that Raviv never studied at a yeshiva associated with Kach,' said Kach leader Baruch Marzel. 'His behavior towards Jews and Arabs was inconsistent with our approach. We would never call another Jew a Nazi. He came to us and asked us to join in a national union of right wing groups. We turned him down. We would never cause the kind of damage to the community that he did.'"

Maariv, 11/24/95
"Kach member Tsuriel Popovich witnessed Raviv in action. 'I saw him beat an old Arab senseless for no reason. If an Arab looked at him or his group, he risked his life. Raviv was causing a lot of trouble for us because we all suffered the stigma he was creating.'"

Kach's spiritual leader, Rabbi Meir Kahane, was assassinated five years before Rabin (to the week), and in equally suspicious circumstances. The campaign of incitement against him in the years leading up to his murder also duplicated the atmosphere leading to the Rabin assassination. But while Rabin was portrayed as a saint after his demise by the Israeli media, Kahane continued to be vilified. Thus Raviv, by dressing his actors in Kach costumes, was simply exploiting an existing public image.

But Amir was not a member of Kach. Once the decision to assassinate Rabin was taken, probably in mid-September, the conspirators went into full gear to turn Amir into a member of the meanest, craziest anti-government organization of them all, Eyal.

To do so, once again Eitan Oren was called into action. On September 22, a month and a half before Rabin's demise, Channel One broadcast Oren's report of an Eyal swearing-in ceremony at the grave of Zionism's founder Theodore Herzl.

Eran Agelbo told me, "Raviv's little play was so ridiculous we spent much of the time laughing. Oren filmed us for over 45 minutes and edited it down to ten minutes for television. My lawyer tried to get the uncut tape from Channel One but no one would hand it over and the police refused to confiscate it."

Maariv, 11/24/95
"An 18-year-old Haredi boy who participated in the swearing-in ceremony recalls, 'None of the participants were Eyal members because Eyal didn't exist except for Raviv and Agelbo.'"

In Eitan Oren's report, a hooded boy holding a gun vows to kill anybody, Jew or Arab, who stands in the way of Eyal's objectives. The director, producer, and scriptwriter were all Avishai Raviv.

Says the Haredi boy: "I arrived at 7:00 in the evening and saw Raviv distributing ski masks to the others. He told us what to do, what to say, where to stand. Agelbo told me, 'You have a nice voice, you swear everyone in.'

"I don't know what Eitan Oren thought, but he knew the whole thing was staged. There was one scene where Raviv demonstrated how he beat new members to make them confess if they were with the Shabak. It looked so absurd that we all burst out laughing. It's no shock that Eitan Oren didn't keep that scene in his film."

Yediot Ahronot, 26/11/95
"Police arrested Eran Agelbo and Mosh Erinfeld for their participation in an Eyal swearing-in ceremony filmed by Eitan Oren and broadcast on Channel One on September 22. In the ceremony, new members vowed to 'spill the

blood of Arabs and Jews who aren't Jews' as well as to break into Orient House in Jerusalem."

Maariv, 11/24/95
"During a previous swearing-in ceremony, Avishai Raviv left two minutes before two squad cars of police arrived to arrest the participants..."

One question remains: how did Eyal get so much television coverage when it was totally out of proportion to the group's actual influence or strength?

A good question, never answered. Another one: How can we explain Eitan Oren's behavior if he wasn't working directly for the Shabak? An associate of Oren's believes, "He is such an ideologue that he got ethically unbalanced, believing he was doing the wrong thing for the right cause."

Perhaps, but someone at Channel One assigned Oren to create Eyal out of nothing and Moti Kirschenbaum approved the broadcasts of Oren's raw, lying disinformation.

With just a few weeks to go before the assassination, it was vital that Amir himself be filmed. So...

Yediot Ahronot, 11/20/95
"A patrol through Hebron, which included Yigal Amir, made the news. The group first broke windows of Arab houses and then smashed the camera of a Palestinian news photographer."

After this little incident, and just two weeks before the assassination, Yigal Amir went to an anti-government demonstration in Efrat and made sure the cameras captured him being taken away by the police kicking and screaming. That clip was shown on Channel One less than four hours after Rabin was murdered. The station was ready with the evidence. And the next day, Channel One was prepared to blame the "anti-peace" community—or more than half the country—for Rabin's death.

The public immediately accepted that Amir assassinated Rabin because he was a member of the extremist Eyal group. What they were not told was that Eyal was created by the Shabak and Channel One. If they had been so informed, Amir's political motive would have become most suspicious.

5
ה

HOW DID THEY MISS AMIR AT THE RALLY?

One of the questions the media asked after the assassination is how the Shabak missed identifying Amir in the sterile area where he "shot" Rabin. The first answer given by the Shabak was that because of the thick crowd, it was impossible to pick out Amir.

The "amateur film," purportedly made by Ronnie Kempler, put that lie to rest. Amir is shown standing alone by a potted plant for long minutes without another soul in sight for yards around him. The only people who are filmed talking to him are two uniformed policemen.

Under normal circumstances, the Shabak would have prevented Amir from getting anywhere near the rally itself—and had he somehow gained access to the sterile area, he would have been apprehended on the spot—because the Shabak had a lot of information that Amir was planning to assassinate Rabin.

Take the famous case of Shlomi Halevy, a reserve soldier in the IDF's Intelligence Brigade and a fellow student of Amir's at Bar Ilan University. After being informed that Amir was talking about killing Rabin, he reported the information to his superior officer in the brigade. He told Halevy to go to the police immediately. Halevy told them that "a short Yemenite in Eyal was boasting that he was going to assassinate Rabin." The police took Halevy very seriously and transferred his report to the Shabak—where it wasn't "discovered" until three days after Rabin's assassination.

The weekly newsmagazine *Yerushalayim* on 9/22/96 managed to convince Halevy to give his first interview since the discovery of his report and the subsequent media fallout. The magazine noted,

"Halevy's and other reports of Amir's intentions, which gathered dust in Shabak files have fueled numerous conspiracy theories... After the uproar, Halevy went into hiding.

'Shlomi Halevy, if you did the right thing why have you hidden from the public?'

'The assassination is a sore point with the Shabak. They're big and I'm little. I don't know what they could do to me.'"

Halevy was the most publicized case because as a soldier in the Intelligence Brigade, the Shabak was absolutely required to take his evidence seriously as did the police. But Halevy was not the only informant.

Yediot Ahronot, 11/12/95
"A number of weeks before the Rabin assassination, the Shabak received information about the existence of Yigal Amir and his intention to murder Yitzhak Rabin."

Yediot Ahronot was informed that one of the Eyal activists arrested last week was interrogated for being a possible co-conspirator with Yigal Amir because the assassin's brother, Haggai, had mentioned him in his own interrogation.

At the beginning of his interrogation, the suspect broke out into bitter tears and told a tale that was initially viewed as tongue in cheek by the interrogators. Weeks before the murder, the suspect heard Amir speak his intentions and he was shocked. He was torn between informing the authorities and betraying his fellows, so he chose a middle route. He would give away Amir's intentions without naming him.

After some hesitation, he informed a police intelligence officer about Amir's plan in detail, stopping just short of identifying him or his address. He told where Amir studied and described him as a "short, dark Yemenite with curly hair."

The description was passed along the police communications network and classified as important. The information was also passed to the Shabak, which subsequently took a statement from the suspect. Because he was in a delicate position, neither the police or Shabak pressed him further.

While interrogated, the suspect named the police and Shabak officers and his story checked out. He was then released. Shabak officials confirmed that the man had previously given them a description of Amir and his plan to murder Rabin.

Maariv, 19/11/95
"Hila Frank knew Amir well from her studies at Bar Ilan. After the assassination, she hired a lawyer and told him that she had heard Amir state his intention to murder Rabin well before the event. As a member of the campus Security Committee, she organized anti-government demonstrations."

Thus, she was torn between exposing Amir's intentions and the interests of the state. To overcome the dilemma, she passed on her information to Shlomi Halevy, a reserve soldier in the Intelligence Brigade who promised that it would be given to the right people.

Yerushalayim, 11/17/95

"Why wasn't a drawing of Amir based on Halevy's description distributed to the Prime Minister's security staff? Why didn't they interrogate other Eyal activists to discover who the man threatening to kill the prime minister was?"

Yediot Ahronot, 11/10/95

"A month and a half before the assassination, journalist Yaron Kenner pretended to be a sympathizer and spent two days at a study Sabbath in Hebron organized by Yigal Amir...

'Who organized this event?' I asked. He pointed to Yigal Amir... He had invited 400 and over 540 arrived. This caused organizational havoc.

"When Amir spoke, people quieted down, testifying to some charisma. On the other hand, his soft tone and unimpressive stature wouldn't have convinced anyone to buy even a popsicle on a hot day from him."

Maariv, 12/12/95

"During his 'Identity Weekends,' hundreds of people heard Amir express his radical thoughts, amongst which were his biblical justifications for the murder of Rabin."

Yediot Ahronot, 11/24/95

"Yigal Amir turned into an object of attention for the Shabak beginning six months ago when he started organizing study weekends in Kiryat Arba and they requested a report on him. Raviv prepared the report."

Maariv, 11/24/95

"A carful of Bar Ilan students were driving from Tel Aviv when they heard the announcement of Rabin's shooting on the radio. They played a game, each thinking of five people who might have done it. Yigal Amir was on all their lists."

How could the Shabak have missed Yigal Amir at the rally unless they did so on purpose? Yigal Amir did not keep his intentions to assassinate Rabin a secret. He told many hundreds of people gathered at his study weekends and seems to have told everyone within hearing distance at Bar Ilan University.

Besides the question of Amir's most un-murderer-like desire to let the world know his plans, we must ask why the Shabak didn't apprehend him. They knew about him. The proof is indisputable. Two people, one within Eyal, the other a soldier in the Intelligence Brigade told them. Their own agent Avishai Raviv heard his threats, along with hundreds of other people at the study weekends and reported them to his superiors.

So why didn't they arrest him well before the rally, outside the rally or within the sterile zone? Because wittingly or not, Yigal Amir was working for the Shabak.

In early September, 1994, the folks responsible for the Rabin assassination sting conducted a wide-ranging practice round. Seventeen Jews were arrested and held without charge for days. Later the Shabak and police proudly proclaimed that they had busted the Vengeance Underground, a Jewish militia which planned to stage terror attacks against Arab villages and against the bastion of the PLO in Jerusalem, Orient House. The seventeen were charged with conspiracy to commit murder. There was an immediate problem with the conspiracy charge; none of the accused knew each other. The only thing they had in common was being framed by Reserve Brigadier General Yisrael Blumental of the IDF's Hebron Brigade and Shabak agent, Yves Tibi.

Of the seventeen, the most publicized case was against Lieutenant Oren Edri, who was arrested while serving in Lebanon and charged with supplying explosives and training to the alleged underground. His real crime, like all the others, was associating with the Jews of Hebron. He was incarcerated for two months in a vermin-filled cell; when his parents visited him for the first time after his arrest, they were utterly horrified to see that his face was severely rat-bitten.

Other arrests were nearly as scandalous. One example:

> Blumental gave Uri Baruch blueprints for making a rifle silencer and Baruch was arrested the next day for planning to construct silencers for the underground. The proof was Blumental's planted evidence.

Eventually all charges were dropped against Edri and Baruch as they were for another 13 conspirators. The only members of the phony underground who stood trial were two brothers Yehoyada and Eitan Kahalani. On June 8, 1995, I met with the attorney who represented their appeal; he was kind enough to supply me with secret and guarded internal documents of the Police and Shabak on condition that he be referred to as "the attorney" and not by name. The attorney explains,

> "In February 1996, the Kahalani brothers were sentenced to 12 years each in prison. This came as a complete shock to almost everyone in the legal field. I decided to try and cheer the boys up by offering to prepare an

appeal pro bono. I became totally dismayed when it was rejected and drew some conclusions.

"The first is that the case was directly connected to the Rabin assassination. The same people in charge of Avishai Raviv and the frameup of Yigal Amir, also framed the Kahalani brothers. Yves Tibi took his orders from Eli Barak, head of the Jewish Department of the Shabak. And Kalo and Gillon were Barak's superiors."

What the attorney did not mention was that Defense Minister General Yitzhak Rabin was the ultimate superior officer of the Shabak and must have been all too aware of the operation which led to the imprisonment of the Kahalani brothers.

The story of one of the greatest miscarriage of justice in Israeli history begins with an egg smuggling scam. Because of corrupt marketing of produce in Israel, food products, including eggs, are very overpriced. Tibi, who lived in the Hebron suburb of Kiryat Arba, went into business with the Kahalani brothers smuggling eggs—buying them from West Bank Arab producers, at a fraction of the cost of Israeli eggs, and smuggling them into Israel proper.

On September 2, 1994, the brothers went scouting routes out of the West Bank in preparation for their new business. For that reason they were driving through obscure West Bank villages—proof, contended the Shabak, that they were actually planning a massacre in one of them.

On their way back to Kiryat Arba, their truck mysteriously broke down and could not climb the hill into Jerusalem. The brothers called Tibi, explained their dilemma and asked to borrow his car. He agreed and everyone met in Jerusalem at 2:00 PM. The Kahalani brothers drove away in Tibi's car and at 2:13 passed through the nearby Arab village within Jerusalem called Batir. At 2:15, they were stopped by a Shabak jeep waiting in ambush. They were forced out of the car at gunpoint and the vehicle was searched. Two M-16 automatic rifles were found tightly wrapped in a blanket. A police squad car arrived shortly after and the brothers were arrested.

They were held in a Shabak lockup without charge and without the right to see a lawyer for a week and a half. Ten days later, on September 12, they were finally charged with the attempted murder of an Arab named Ziad Shami who complained to the police that while riding a bicycle to work, the brothers had attempted to shoot him, but the rifle misfired. The Shabak had searched for him in Batir to "see if he was hurt or not." A week later, Shami's cousin also complained to the police that "settlers had tried to shoot me." It wasn't until September 15 that the Shabak explained that it had rigged the brothers' rifles to prevent them from shooting in order to catch the attempted murderers red-handed. If this sounds like an early rehearsal for the Rabin assassination, it probably was.

The literature of political assassinations has its rehearsal precedents. President Ford was shot at first by Squeaky Fromme for ecological reasons and within days by Sarah Moore on a similar pretext. John Lennon was murdered a month before the attempted assassination of Ronald Reagan in 1982. Lennon's murderer, Mark David Chapman explained that he was Holden Caulfield of *Catcher In The Rye* and the public accepted this unbelievable excuse for Lennon's murder. The dry run successful, Reagan's attempted assassin claimed he was trying to impress actress Jodie Foster and the public bought it, as expected.

Rabin's assassins were trying out sting operations to see if patsies could be charged without cause and imprisoned without a major public outcry. With the help of the police and courts, the system worked. Most of the Israeli public were gullible and apathetic enough to ignore the sting and all its implications for their civil rights.

I asked the attorney if the plot didn't backfire in the case of the rat-bitten Lieutenant Edri. "Was anyone in the Shabak charged with the wrongful arrest of Edri?" he asked in return. "They got way with it and learned that the Israeli public wouldn't protest even the atrocities an innocent soldier was subjected to. The Shabak was confident it could get away with any sting."

And with good reason, if they managed to get the Kahalani brothers imprisoned against all the rules of jurisprudence. The attorney showed me some sensitive documents. The first was from the police ballistics expert Bernard Shechter, who examined the alleged rifles and ammunition of the Kahalani brothers just as, a year later, he would examine the weapons and ammunition of the Amir brothers.

The date on Shechter's report is September 1, 1994, one day before the rifles were found in Tibi's car while driven by the brothers. Shechter reports that he fired the rifles and they were in good working order. Allow me to stress the obvious. The incriminating M-16s were in the hands of the police on September 1; how did the Kahalani brothers get them the very next day? There can be little doubt: the answer is, the rifles were planted.

Next, the attorney showed me a memo dated September 2, 1994, marked secret, from the Shabak to the police. The police wanted the rifles turned over to them immediately for examination. The Shabak refused, citing unnamed security considerations. The attorney next showed me a report from Bernard

Shechter dated September 29. Finally, after 27 days, the police tested the weapons and found them to be defective. Needless to say, just like the case of Yigal Amir's alleged bullets which were unaccounted for before the police tested them, the chain of evidence regarding the Kahalani brothers' rifles was completely broken.

But that didn't bother the judges. Again, as was the case during Yigal Amir's trial, the attorney explains, "The court said it was not interested in who gave the brothers the weapons, just who pulled the trigger."

There was another problem with the state's case—initially there were no fingerprints on the rifles. The Shabak explained that was because the brothers wiped them clean. Thus, the Shabak had the Kahalani brothers attempting to shoot an Arab, wiping the weapons clean of fingerprints and then tightly wrapping them in a blanket before being apprehended less than two minutes later.

The scenario didn't stand the test of probability, so the Shabak came up with a new version. Yes, there actually were fingerprints on the weapon—but not of the Kahalani brothers. Somehow they had wiped out their prints and left other people's intact. The police would get to the bottom of this: they tested all the prints of the arrested underground members. The attorney showed me the police document. All members' prints were examined except those of the Shabak snitch who most likely placed the rifles in his car—Yves Tibi.

Shocking? It's just the veritable tip of the iceberg. Here are some of the inconsistencies listed by the attorney in his appeal to the court.

- Why did the Shabak have to go looking for a victim? No one complained against the brothers until ten days later when the Shabak went looking for a complainant, "To make certain he wasn't hurt." Why, asked the attorney, "should the Shabak think he was hurt if they rigged the rifles so they wouldn't fire?" The first thing the Shabak officers claimed they told Shami was, "Don't worry. We're here to protect you from the settlers."

- Shami had been previously arrested by the Shabak on numerous occasions for violent activity and had been imprisoned by them twice. They were well known to each other. Shami would have needed little convincing to give false testimony if he thought he was helping to put away settlers. Shami claimed first that one of the brothers pulled the trigger of the rifle, he heard a "tik" sound and saw the cartridge fall to the ground. The story was patently absurd since a cartridge minus the bullet will not be expelled, if the trigger is pulled, without firing, so he changed his story. In his second statement to the police, Shami claimed one brother fired from a bending position behind the car and he couldn't hear the "tik" and didn't see a bullet fall.

- In his first police statement, Shami said he could identify the brothers. In his second, he was tripped up by the interrogator who asked which one wore the glasses. After he answered, Shami was told that neither wore glasses. He then admitted that he could not identify the suspects. Neither could the two Shabak agents who awaited them at the ambush. So, the police decided to sidestep the problem by not putting the brothers in a lineup. In court, the police investigator explained that arranging a lineup was "logistically difficult." As was the simple task of interrogating the subjects. The police actually disagreed in court about which officer interrogated which brother.

- When asked why it took ten days to make a police complaint against his attempted murderer, Shami told the court, "I took it as an everyday incident." Now, even in the politically charged atmosphere of Israel, being shot at point blank is not an everyday incident. So, someone decided to beef up Shami's case by bringing in an employee of his who testified that the next day, Shami had told him what happened. But the defense had produced Shami's work card which proved he had gone to work on the 2nd, just after the alleged murder attempt. Why didn't he tell his employee about the incident that day? The employee then changed his story. Now Shami did tell him the same day.

- Why did Shami's cousin complain to the police on September 9 that two settlers pulled a gun on him? The Kahalani brothers were already locked up, so it wasn't they who did it. Was the little village of Batir targeted by settlers who were terrorizing the citizenry with failed murder attempts? Did the Shabak or police follow up on the complaint or was it a simple, perverse attempt by a family member to save Shami from perjury charges?

- Shami reported that he had left his bicycle on the spot and run away. The two Shabak ambushers reported that the bicycle was gone and that Shami must have rode off on it. To explain away this problem, Shami insisted that as he was running away, he flagged down a Peugeot van driven by a friend, returned to the crime scene and picked up his bicycle. The Shabak ambushers had to have seen the Peugeot van if it existed. And Shami could not name the friend who drove the van so he again altered his story to the police. This time the Peugeot was driven by a stranger.

- Shami insisted that one of his assailants held a rifle to him. The Shabak ambushers admitted they never saw anyone actually holding a rifle.

- The policemen in the squad car accompanying the Shabak jeep at the ambush somehow did not witness the arrest of the brothers. The squad car followed the jeep but the view was hampered by the "dust kicked up by the jeep." By the time the dust settled, the policemen saw the brothers held on the ground at gunpoint, the rifles in the blanket beside them. The dust, then, took at least two minutes to settle.

- Shami told the police the first thing the Kahalani brothers asked him was, "What's the time?" When asked in court the first thing they asked, he replied, "Do you have any money?"

- Police Warrant Officer Zeiger testified that a bullet clip was pulled out of the brothers' backpack at the time of the arrest. Unfortunately for Zeiger, no fingerprints of the brothers were found on the clip. Further, the police log of 9/2/94 reports that the clip was found in the defendants' home. In short, officer Zeiger was caught lying. But then, who wasn't?

The verdict of this ridiculous case was to be read on November 6, 1995, but it was delayed until November 15 because of the murder of Rabin on November 4. On November 15, the court found the Kahalani brothers guilty of attempted murder.

"That verdict," says the attorney, "was directly related to the assassination. If the Kahalani brothers sting operation did not result in a conviction, people might have started asking questions about Yigal Amir. I asked associates in the Shabak how the brothers could have been convicted in the face of such an abundance of obviously doctored evidence. They told me there was just one possible answer,

> "At the highest levels of the Shabak, there was a policy to delegitimize the settlers in order to justify their forced removal at some stage of the peace process."

The opponents of the secret and deceitful "peace" process were thus to be turned into savage murderers. And if they weren't so in reality, then murderers would have to be manufactured. It didn't matter how much injustice it took, so long as the opponents of the peace process were viewed as barbarians by as much of the voting public as possible.

With this strategy in mind, Rabin was supposedly assassinated by a right-wing Sephardic Jew who sympathized with the settler movement. The day after, the roundup of hundreds of Jewish opponents of "peace" began and barely anyone complained. Within several weeks, the Israeli army pulled out of six West Bank regions without so much as one protest sign blocking the way.

In February 1996, the Kahalani brothers were supposed to appear for sentencing. Only one, Eitan, arrived. Yehodaya was not capable of hearing his twelve-year sentence. A few weeks earlier, he was transferred to another cell block. He was talking to his mother on the phone when an iron pipe smashed down on his skull, crushing it. He went into a deep coma from which it appeared, at first, he might never escape. His last words to his mother were, "They put me in here with murderers."

7

ר̄

FROM THE MOUTHS
OF THE SHABAK

After the assassination, the head of the Shabak, Carmi Gillon, his two officers in charge of Jewish radicals and their agent, Avishai Raviv, found themselves in deep, hot water. The post-assassination plan hit a snag; someone had leaked the truth about Raviv.

Gillon's first step was to appoint his own internal commission of inquiry, but the public saw through the trick. This forced the government to appoint its own commission of inquiry headed by Chief Justice Shamgar who made a show of trying to get to the truth. He turned up the heat by sending letters to seven Shabak officers, including Gillon and Jewish Activities Department head Khezi Kalo but pointedly not his colleague, Eli Barak, who oversaw the Raviv operation. He informed each that they were liable for criminal prosecution. Some of their testimony leaked out to the public, though 30% remains buried in a vault for supposed state-security reasons. But from what little did escape from the mouths of the Shabak, we get a hint of the mentality of the men at the top charged with protecting Yitzhak Rabin from Yigal Amir.

From Carmi Gillon's 1990 master's thesis:
"There is a radicalization of the ideological law violations of the extreme right regarding the amount of activity and the force of this activity. Israeli society displays tolerance toward ideological lawbreakers of the extreme right and this grants, albeit belatedly, legitimacy to these activities."

Yediot Ahronot, 11/10/95
"A group of journalists met Carmi Gillon at the end of August. Among other things, he painted a portrait of a potential Jewish assassin of the Prime Minister. Without knowing it, he described Yigal Amir perfectly. He would be someone who didn't live in the territories, said the Shabak head, he will not be a joiner but an almost wise loner, who lives in Herzlea."

From Carmi Gillon's master's thesis:
"The process of extremism in Israeli society is creating individuals who will ignore danger in pursuit of their goals."

Yediot Ahronot, 11/20/95

"Quotes from the head of the Shabak at the Shamgar Commission are teaching us his defense. He is calling Amir a 'lone nut' who awoke one day and decided to murder the prime minister without anyone's help. He claims nuts like these are very hard to identify so the murder was not caused by an 'intelligence breakdown.'"

This is a very problematic defense. Although Amir has testified that he worked alone, other evidence suggests that three or four other people were in on the secret. Amir was not exactly anti-social. Gillon's "lone nut" theory doesn't make sense.

Yediot Ahronot, 11/24/95

"The head of the Shabak had no doubt who the assassin was. The moment he was informed of the close-range shooting by long distance phone, his first reaction was, 'It was a Jew.'"

Avraham Rotem, former head of Personal Security for the Shabak asks himself a few questions:

Maariv, 11/10/95

"Where was the head of the Shabak last Saturday night? Abroad. What was he doing there? Not known. Something urgent. What's more urgent than protecting the life of the prime minister? He didn't know someone was going to murder Rabin.

"Aah, he didn't know? So why is it written in the papers that a few months ago he warned Rabin that someone from the extreme right was planning to assassinate him? And then he went to the heads of the political parties to give the same warning and request that they prevent incitement to murder? You can't tell the prime minister that someone is going to murder him and then go back to routine security procedures."

It looks like Gillon knew the assassination was coming sometime around early September when he warned Rabin, political party heads and journalists of an impending murder of the prime minister by an almost-wise loner who doesn't live in the territories.

Forty-eight hours before the assassination Gillon felt impelled to fly to Paris, despite pleas from subordinates not to leave before the rally, on unknown "urgent" business. When told of the shooting, he knew immediately that a Jew did it.

Unfortunately for him, he stuck to the original plan and, taking the Warren Commission findings to heart, he defended himself by calling Amir a "lone nut." But like Oswald, Amir was neither a loner or a nut.

Despite this flimsy defense, and without asking the hard questions about his uncannily accurate assassination predictions or what he was doing in Paris, Shamgar let Gillon off with a wrist slap.

Agent Kalo

He is the most mysterious Shabak figure surrounding the assassination, even his first name was never leaked into the media. It is known that Eli Barak, as head of the Jewish Department of the Shabak, ran Aviv, but no one has properly delineated Kalo's role. All we know is that he was Barak's immediate superior.

> *Maariv*, 12/18/95
> The Shamgar Commission has begun examining the contradictions between police testimony and that of Agent Kalo...They are asking how the Shabak reacted to information coming out of Bar Ilan University and why the Shabak was ignorant of the Shabbat activities in Judea and Samaria organized by Yigal Amir with Avishai Raviv.

> *Yediot Ahronot*, 11/22/95
> According to the head of the Department of Jewish Activities (Kalo) during six hours of testimony at the Shamgar Commission, the Shabak requested that Raviv supply them with an overview of Amir's activities three months before the assassination.

Raviv returned from his field duties and told them of Amir's intention to harm Arabs. Kalo testified, "Raviv didn't know Amir's real intentions and did not inform us of his plans to harm Jews, including the Prime Minister."

> *Maariv*, 12/19/95
> Among those most surprised by the warning letter from Shamgar was Kheshin, who believes the cause of Rabin's assassination was a security, not intelligence breakdown. He believes the warning to him was totally unjustified.

The head of the Jewish Activities Department claims he knew nothing of Yigal Amir's threats to Rabin at Bar Ilan University and received a report from his agent, Avishai Raviv, three months before the murder, which completely ignored those very threats—threats which Raviv had heard on numerous occasions.

Instead he was told Amir wanted to beat up Arabs. This was patently false. The frail Amir refused to participate in any of the many Arab-beating forays into Hebron lead by Raviv until once, shortly before the assassination when he was fortuitously filmed in action.

Can anyone believe this story? If it's true, Raviv was deliberately hiding the truth about Amir from Kalo while other subordinates purposely kept the intelligence from Bar Ilan University away from his prying eyes.

Eli Barak

He was the head of The Non-Arab Anti-Subversive Unit of the Shabak, usually called the Jewish Department. Kalo was his superior officer hinting that the Jewish Activities Department was separate from his own. Because the thirty percent of the Shamgar Commission report hidden from the public includes information on the Shabak's departmental infrastructure, the exact nature of the chain of command is not known. And because Shamgar excluded Barak from testifying in open session for reasons known as coverup, not much of what he has to say has been released. But some testimony made it to the light of day.

> *Yediot Ahronot* 11/20/95
> "According to the London newspaper *The Observer,* high Israeli security officials claim that officers of the Shabak knew about Yigal Amir's intention to murder Yitzhak Rabin. The highest ranking officer who knew was Eli Barak, head of the Jewish Department, who didn't take Amir's 'ridiculous plans' seriously. The newspaper doesn't explain why Barak didn't pass on Amir's threats to the head of the Shabak and that the answer to this will have to come out at the commission of inquiry."

> *Maariv,* 11/27/95
> "Eli Barak, head of the department which deals with Jewish extremists, testified that Avishai Raviv didn't know that Yigal Amir intended to murder Yitzhak Rabin. He only reported that he was an activist at Bar Ilan University. According to Barak, Amir decided on his own to murder Rabin and that no one could have stopped him."

The former head of the Mossad, Committee member Tzvi Zamir, asked Barak to explain why the Shabak didn't act on Shlomi Halevy's report to the police that a short, Yemenite member of Eyal was threatening Rabin. The committee stressed that, because Halevi was a soldier of the Intelligence Brigade, red lights should have lit up.

Barak's answer was never published. The little tidbit we have of Barak suggests that he coordinated testimony with Gillon and pushed the lone nut theory. He also seems to have had a good talk with Kalo, but with a difference. While Kalo claimed to have been ignorant of Amir's campus radicalism, Raviv chose to inform Barak about it. However, both agree that agent Raviv didn't know Amir had any plans to murder Rabin.

Avishai Raviv

We know that Avishai Raviv was a Shabak agent from at least 1987, when the deacon of Tel Aviv University, Itamal Rabinovitch, tried to expel him for extremist activities. Prime Minister Shamir sent his aide, Yossi Achimeir, to intervene with Rabinovitch on Raviv's behalf. Thus, at the time of the assassination Raviv had been in the Shabak for at least eight years and probably had risen to high rank.

But finding quotes from him that aren't staged extremism is tough. In November 1996, the news magazine *Kol Ha'ir* tracked him down to his secret place of work in a Tel Aviv institute for autistic children. Why he has to work at all is a mystery, but presumably autistic children won't recognize him. He didn't say much to the reporter but admitted, "No one would believe what I know and can't tell." For presumably if he did, he would disappear for good.

We also know that he lied at the trial of Haggai Amir. He told the court, "I never worked for or was associated with the Shabak." Finally, we also know the court system is rigged because it accepted the perjured testimony without protest.

THE PLAN THAT
WASN'T USED

The Shabak's explanation for the failure to protect Rabin at Kings of Israel Square was that they had no contingency plans to protect the Prime Minister against a lone gunman. The reasoning that no one can stop a determined maverick assassin was employed by Shabak chief, Carmi Gillon, and it flowed down from him through the ranks.

Seventeen months after the assassination, the excuse was shattered to bits in an interview for *Anashim* magazine by two former officers of the Shabak's personal security unit, Tuvia Livneh and Yisrael Shai. The opening paragraph reads,

> "For the first time since the assassination of Yitzhak Rabin, two former officers of the unit assigned to protect him are speaking out. They are aghast at the behavior of their successors in the unit who failed to prevent the murder and the ease with which the assassin, Yigal Amir, entered the sterile zone and shot at the former prime minister from arm's length. For the past seventeen months, not a day has passed when the thought does not occur to them that the murder wouldn't have happened had they not stood down.
>
> "'With us, Rabin wouldn't have been murdered,' says Tuvia Livneh.
>
> "'When Yisrael and I heard the news of the murder we became infuriated at the fact that there was a contingency plan for just such an attempt, which we practiced endless times.'"

The report continues,

> "This is not a case of wisdom after the fact, but scandalous wisdom well before the event, which is being published for the first time: when the two commanded the unit at the beginning of the 1990s, they prepared a detailed contingency plan for a political assassination at Kings of Israel Square, including the possibility that the assassin would act from the exit stairs behind the stage, precisely where Yigal Amir waited for Yitzhak Rabin. The plan was transferred to field command where it was practiced in dry runs."

So much for Carmi Gillon's insistence that no contingency plan existed for an assassination attempt at Kings of Israel Square. An exact contingency plan existed, so exact in fact, that one wonders if it was used in reverse.

Shabak officers had rehearsed an assassination attempt "endless times" at the precise spot Amir awaited Rabin. Not only were they not likely caught off guard, they were uniquely prepared to prevent the assassination... if they had wanted to. The article continues,

> "What pains Livneh and Shai no less, is that Amir remained alive and well despite shooting three bullets in peace and quiet. A basic principle of theirs was that even if an anonymous killer penetrates the first line of defense and gets off a shot one way or another at the prime minister or anyone else, it will be his last shot. Immediately after Amir's first shot, the prime minister's bodyguards had to take two actions, both of which had been rehearsed an infinite number of times: first, the prime minister had to be covered by his guards' bodies and rushed away, second, the assassin had to be shot.
>
> "Films of other political assassinations, for instance those of Ronald Reagan and Anwar Sadat, showed that the bodyguards followed those rules, but in Israel, which is considered an exporter of superb security systems throughout the world, the killer managed to shoot the prime minister three times, one shot more damaging than the next, and he remained standing happily on his feet, alive throughout."

Anashim is not the first publication to ask why Rabin's bodyguards didn't shoot Amir. The only plausible answer is that they were told not to ahead of time. What makes this report especially significant is that it comes from the highest ranks of the Shabak and it insists that Rabin was shot *three* times, each shot more damaging.

This coincides with information we will examine later: the announcement of Health Minister Ephraim Sneh on the night of the murder that Rabin was shot three times, including once in the chest, and it corroborates a brief to the Supreme Court of Israel in July 1996 from a witness who testified that an Ichilov Hospital pathologist told him he found three bullet holes in Rabin's body.

The reporter says to Livneh, "For years you trained your people to kill the assassin but when the real thing happened, they didn't do a thing." Livneh replies, "I suppose that when an unknown man shouted, 'They're blanks,' he stopped the guards in their tracks."

Livneh is looking for an excuse to explain the failures of the bodyguards. What he finds is a non-starter. However, he does acknowledge that it was not

Amir who did the shouting. This corroborates Amir's own testimony. Shortly after Amir was arrested, a police interrogator asked him, "Did you shout that the bullets were blanks?"

"Why would I do that?" Amir replied.

"To throw the bodyguards off your trail. To temporarily confuse them."

"An interesting idea," Amir replied. "But I didn't do it."

In fact, as will be illustrated, *"Srak, srak,"* meaning "They're blanks, blanks," was far from the only thing shouted after the shooting. Bodyguards yelled a variety of similar sentences including, "It was nothing," "It's an exercise," "It's not real," "Caps," "Toy gun," etc.

But Livneh continues with his thesis, "I stress that I have no personal information, but it's reasonable to assume that one of Amir's co-conspirators, whether known or unknown, stood near him in the crowd and aided him in this way. Or maybe it was Amir, after all."

Since Amir could not have shouted from eight or nine different locations, it wasn't he. If there were other conspirators, they would have had to have been bodyguards. The article continues.

> "Livneh and Shai were pleased when the Shamgar Commission was formed and waited patiently to be called to testify. Both were considered the leading experts on personal security in the country; both served for years in the unit and were the personal bodyguards of such central figures as Golda Meir, Moshe Dayan, Ezer Weizmann and of Rabin himself during his first term in office; both knew the service inside out and rose through the ranks until they became its commanders, first Livneh, then Shai.
>
> "But the Shamgar Commission ignored them completely. Both have strong suspicions about why. However, at this point, they refuse to publicly elaborate."

The most likely reason, of course, is that Livneh and Shai would have given honest testimony that would have destroyed the credibility of the version of events given by the Shabak officers who failed to protect Rabin.

Livneh concludes with a hint of what he would have testified:

> "There was nothing new about the murder, nothing we hadn't taken into account in the past. The fact that the murderer was able to complete his mission was the humiliating fault of those responsible for personal security that night. That's all I'm willing to say."

And yet not one Shabak officer responsible for Rabin's security was tried, court martialled, or imprisoned. The worst punishment meted out was forced resignation. And that only led to a career advancement for the ultimate head of Rabin's personal security, Carmi Gillon. He left the Shabak and was later appointed to head the Foreign Ministry's negotiations with the Palestinians.

After negotiations, Gillon turned down the appointment but the fact remains that the man who offered him the job was the Likud Foreign Minister, David Levy.

The coverup continued into the new government.

9 THE KEMPLER FILM

Almost two months after the Rabin assassination, Israelis were shocked to read in their newspapers that an amateur film of the event would be shown on Channel Two news. The filmmaker was announced as a Polish tourist with a long, unpronounceable name. However, this story changed the day of the broadcast. The filmmaker was, in fact, an Israeli named Roni Kempler.

There were obvious questions asked by the public. Why had he waited a month to show the film when he would have been a few million dollars richer had he sold it to the world networks the day following the assassination? In his sole television appearance the night his film was broadcast, Kempler explained he wasn't interested in making money. What else could he say?

It was quickly discovered that Kempler was no ordinary citizen. He worked for the State Comptroller's Office and was a bodyguard in the army reserves.

It is an extremely rare occurance when the Israeli press publishes an opinion that expresses doubt about the veracity of the Shamgar Commission, which investigated the assassination on behalf of the government. Yet in the aftermath of a most revealing exposé of the testimony of Shabak agents and police officers present near the murder site published by *Maariv* on 9/27/96, two letters were published in response. One was from Labour Knesset Member, Ofir Pines, who admitted he, too, heard numerous security agents shout that the shots which supposedly felled Rabin were blanks. He added rather weakly that in retrospect, perhaps he heard the shouts because he wanted to believe that the bullets weren't real.

A second letter was from Hannah Chen of Jerusalem. She succinctly summarized some of the most blatant suspicions of Roni Kempler. The letter read:

"Allow me to add my doubts about the strange facts surrounding the Rabin assassination. First, it was said that the video filmmaker who captured the murder didn't own his own camera, rather he borrowed one. It's odd that an amateur filmmaker didn't own a camera and, if he borrowed one, then from whom? Why weren't we told what kind of a camera he used? Secondly, no one initially knew that he made the film, that a film of the assassination existed. Does that mean none of the security agents on the scene spotted him filming from a rooftop? And how did the video get to the media? Shouldn't the Shabak have confiscated the film from its owner if this was the only documentary evidence describing the crime? And why didn't the filmmaker voluntarily turn over the film to the police? It is completely uncertain if the film is authentic. In my opinion, it was tampered with. Perhaps people were removed or bullet sounds added. It appears to me that we were all fooled. The filmmaker worked for the Shabak and everything to do with the film and the timing of its release were fake."

Ms. Chen expressed the view of many. Nonetheless, the film, as edited as it obviously was during its two months of non-acknowledgement, is as valuable to solving the Rabin assassination as was the Zapruder film in putting to rest the lone-gunman lie foisted on the American public in the wake of the JFK murder.

One event in particular that was captured on the film is becoming the center of doubt about the veracity of the Shamgar Commission. Before Rabin enters his vehicle, the opposite door closes from inside. To almost everyone who watches that door close, it is certain that someone, perhaps the murderer, was waiting in the Cadillac for Rabin. This is in direct contradiction to the official conclusion that Rabin entered an empty car. But there is more on the Kempler film that contradicts the official findings—much more.

As the fifteen-minute film begins, Yigal Amir looks in the distance and as the television commentator noted, "Seems to be signalling someone." It is not the first time that the possibility of an accomplice was noted. At the Shamgar Commission, police officers, Boaz Eran and Moti Sergei, both testified that Amir spoke with a bearded man in a dark tee-shirt, whom he appeared to know, about 30 minutes before the shooting.

As the film progresses, the viewer realizes that Shabak testimony before Shamgar was very incorrect. One of the primary excuses given for not identifying Amir in the sterile area was because of the crowded situation. To prove the point, the testimony of police officers saying that "another well-known demonstrator, who works for the city, rushed at Rabin and shook his hand," is cited. Amir, then, was not the only anti-Rabin individual in the sterile zone. However, Amir is not filmed in a crowd. He stands for long minutes meters away from anyone else. No one could have missed him had they wanted to see him.

Then, two security officers strike up a conversation with Amir. He was noticed and apparently had something to say to the very people who should have identified and apprehended him.

A few seconds later, Shimon Peres comes down the steps and walks towards the crowd at the barrier. He accepts their good wishes and walks to a spot about a meter and a half opposite the hood of Rabin's car. He is accompanied by four bodyguards, one of whom clearly points to Yigal Amir sitting three meters away opposite them. Peres stops, looks inside the car and begins a conversation with the bodyguards. All now take a good look at the Rabin limousine rear door.

At this point there is a cut. Suddenly Peres is talking to Rabin's driver, Menachem Damti. Damti was nowhere in the screen previously and was likely by his post beside the driver's seat door. The cut was significant, probably of several seconds. There was something the folks who chopped the film didn't want the public to see.

After a hard night at the rally, instead of getting into his car and going home, Peres decided it was more important to examine Rabin's car and have a serious chat with his driver.

Roni Kempler was asked to explain the cut in the film under oath at Yigal Amir's trial. He testified that, "Shimon Peres left and I filmed him as he was supposed to enter his car. But when Shimon Peres stood on the same spot for a long time, he stopped interesting me cinematically. I stopped filming and started again the moment he entered his car."

Kempler's account was wrong in every detail. If the film wasn't cut and he shut off the camera, he decided to turn it back on while Peres was still standing opposite Rabin's car, only now talking to Damti. Many seconds later, he started walking towards his own car. Kempler's testimony was perjured, yet Amir's lawyers, possibly not familiar enough with the film, let him off the hook.

Peres enters his car as Rabin descends the steps. The camera captures the agent at Rabin's rear clearly stopping. He abandons Rabin's back deliberately; a huge gap between him and Rabin opens, allowing Amir a clear shot at the Prime Minister. Amir draws his gun from deep inside his right pocket and the television commentator notes, "Amir is drawing his gun to shoot." Anyone, trained or not, could see that Amir was drawing a gun, and at that point he should have been pounced on. But this was not to be. Instead, he circles a student reporter named Modi Yisrael, draws the gun and shoots.

We now play the murder frame by frame. Rabin has supposedly taken a hollow-point 9mm bullet in his lung, yet he doesn't wince or flinch. He is not even pushed forward by the impact nor does his suit show signs of tearing. Instead, he continues walking forward and turns his head behind him in the direction of the noise.

Three doctors watched this moment with me; Drs. B. and H. asked for anonymity and Dr. Klein of Tel Aviv had no objection to being cited. I asked if Rabin's reaction was medically feasible if he was only hit in the lung or if his backbone was shattered. I was told that if the spine was hit, Rabin would have fallen on the spot. However, in the case of a lung wound, I was told that there are two types of pain reaction, one reflexive, the other delayed. Rabin, did not display the reflexive reaction, which would have most likely meant clutching the arm. Instead, he displayed a startle reaction, painlessly turning his head toward the direction of the shot. The conclusion of the doctors was that Rabin heard a shot, perhaps felt the blast of a blank and turned quickly towards the noise. This was a startle reaction, *and it cannot occur simultaneously with a reflexive pain reaction.*

Rabin takes three or four steps forward, and suddenly the film becomes totally hazy for just under two seconds. A technical expert told me he is convinced the film was deliberately made fuzzy by an artificial process duplicating a sudden, quick movement of the camera. To illustrate his belief, he put his finger on one point, a white reflective light on the windshield, and notes that it stays in the same position while the camera is supposedly moving. But the haze lifts momentarily almost two seconds later and Rabin appears, still standing but a step or two forward. He has taken at least five steps since the shooting. Then the swish returns and within the next round of haze, another shot is heard but not seen.

According to the Shamgar Commission and the judges at Yigal Amir's trial, Yoram Rubin was on top of Rabin lying on the parking lot ground when the second shot was fired. The official version is that after hearing the first shot, Rubin jumps on Rabin and pushes him to the ground. Amir approached Rabin and Rubin and, while being held by at least two other bodyguards, pumped one bullet into Rubin's arm and another into Rabin's spleen. There followed a hiatus in the shooting, during which Rubin thinks to himself, "A defect in the weapon," and then according to Rubin,

> "I shouted at him several times, 'Yitzhak, can you hear me, just me and no one else, goddammit?' He (Rabin) helped me to my feet. That is, we worked together. He then jumped into the car. In retrospect, I find it amazing that a man his age could jump like that."

The author finds it amazing that a man his age with bullets in his lung and spleen could jump at all.

The Kempler film reveals that the whole story is utter hogwash. A famous photo of Rabin being shoved into the car shows up on the film as a flash. At that point, we know Rubin, injured arm and all, is not on the ground, rather he is on his feet holding Rabin. There are 24 frames/second in video film, so timing events is simple. From the time of the second shot to the flash, 4.6 seconds pass. Try repeating, "Yitzhak can you hear me, just me and no one else, goddamit" three times in 4.6 seconds. Then add the hiatus, a hiatus long enough for a man being shot to decide it's safe to get up, and think to yourself "A defect in the weapon." Try all that in 4.6 seconds. Rubin's timing is simply impossible.

Further, Rubin is not filmed on top of Rabin until all shots are fired, and Rabin does not jump into car. The photo of Rubin pulling Rabin into the car disproves that even without the added proof of the Kempler film. Rubin's testimony, to put it mildly, is not born out by the Kempler film.

And now comes the *piece de resistance*, the most haunting moment of the tape. Two seconds before Rabin is placed in the car, the opposite back passenger door slams shut. This segment has been examined and tested by numerous journalists, every shadow on the screen traced, every possible explanation exhausted and in the end it has withstood all scrutiny. Someone, an unknown fourth person, possibly the murderer, was waiting inside the car for Rabin.

When I show this segment to audiences, inevitably I am asked, "Why did they make this film if it's so incriminating?" I reply, "The film convinced the whole country that Amir murdered Rabin. People always say, 'But I saw him do it with my own eyes.' And that is what the film was supposed to do. But the conspirators were so sloppy, they left in the truth. Either they didn't notice it, or they thought no one else would."

So why didn't Yigal Amir's attorneys tear Kempler to bits on the stand or use the film to its maximum advantage? Truth be told, Amir's attorneys either weren't interested enough in his welfare, weren't properly prepared or weren't talented enough to challenge the kangaroo court head on. Take a look at how they handled the issue of the unexplainable closing door.

Defense: "After the event, the back right door of the car was also open."

Kempler: "I filmed what I filmed."

The end, no followup. And it's not that the defense didn't have plenty of ammunition. On the night his film was shown on Channel Two in December 1995, Kempler was interviewed by commentator Rafi Reshef. The fast talking, nervous Kempler was most unbelievable, as the following interview segments show.

Reshef: "Why did you wait so long to release the film to the public?"

Kempler: "A few reasons. I didn't want to be known. Also, I thought it was forbidden to show the film so soon after the murder. The public needed time to digest it as a historic film...But after the Shamgar Commission got it, I kept hearing on the street that I'm the sucker of the country. That really aggravated me, so I got a lawyer and decided to make some money selling it."

How altruistic! What Kempler forgets to mention is that he didn't tell anyone he had filmed the assassination until two weeks later when supposedly he woke up to what he had and sent the Shamgar Commission a registered letter informing them. In the meantime, he was withholding vital evidence from the police.

Reshef: "Did anyone observe you filming?"

Kempler: "Yes, the bodygua...I'm sure I saw (singer) Aviv Gefen look right into my camera."

Kempler almost let slip that the bodyguards were watching him film, and indeed this is apparent on the film itself when, just before the Peres cut, one of the bodyguards turns back and looks directly up to him, but he thought the better of it and switched to a nonsensical fantasy involving a pop singer.

Reshef: "Why did you concentrate so much of the film on the killer?"

Kempler: "I felt there was something suspicious about him. I let my imagination run away with me and felt murder in the air. It wasn't so strong when Peres was there but when Rabin appeared, WOW."

Kempler felt there was an assassination in the air and suspected Amir could be the assassin. This was truly a parapsychological feat but lucky it happened or he wouldn't have bothered focusing in on Amir. And lucky he just happened to be the only cameraman on the balcony overlooking the murder scene. And luckily, it was so dark at the murder scene few amateur cameras could have captured the act.

Reshef: "There has been much speculation why you happened to be the only one in the right place to film the assassination. How do you explain it?"

Kempler: "I felt someone caused me to be in that place."

Reshef: "What, are you a fatalist?"

Nope, a mystic as we shall soon see.

Reshef: "Did anyone try to interfere with you?"

Kempler: "There were undercover officers around. One told me it was alright to film but I had to stop when Rabin appeared."

Now compare the next version of events with what Kempler testified to at Amir's trial.

Kempler: "An undercover policeman came up to me and asked me a few questions and asked to see my ID. I showed it to him and he walked away. He stopped, turned back and shouted, 'What did you say your name was?' I shouted it back. He said, 'Good.' And that was that. The police had all the details of my identity."

So why didn't the police call that night to get the film? What is described is a very friendly encounter, indeed. Here is how the incident was transformed for Amir's trial.

Kempler: "There was an undercover cop who told me not to film. I told him he has no right to tell me not to film. I asked him if something secret was going on? I told him again he has no right to tell me not to film. And if he does it again, I would take down his particulars and issue a complaint to the police."

A rather drastically altered situation. Someone thought that Kempler's explanation to Reshef about why he was permitted to film in such a sensitive security location was too weak, so he painted a new, tougher picture. An updated version of his previous explanation about why he focused in on Amir painted a much goofier portrait.

Kempler: "When I stood on the balcony, I spent a lot of time in the dark and to my regret, my imagination began to work overtime. I begin to imagine many things, even God forbid, a political assassination... I have no explanation why I had this feeling. I'm not sure it wasn't something mystic."

And because of this mysticism, Kempler felt,

"The defendant stood out. I don't know what he did... but I recall he stood out. I can't recall anything other than what I filmed."

Indeed he couldn't because at the beginning of his testimony Kempler says the film shown to the public, "contained no changes or alterations." By the end, he admits, "There are gaps and there are differences."

Why the change of heart? Because Amir's attorneys pointed out some very suspicious contradictions in the film.

This photo of
Rabin being pushed
into the car, clearly
disproves Yoram
Rubin's testimony
that Rabin jumped
into the car.

The doctored Kempler
film still from the front
page of *Yediot Achronot*.
Notice that the right-
handed Amir appears to
be shooting with his left
hand.

1. Rabin
2. Amir
3. Mordi Yisrael
4. Damti, the driver
5. Yoram Rubin

Defense: "We don't hear everything in the film but we hear lots, including shouts. So why don't we hear the shouts of 'They're blanks.'"

Kempler: "Don't ask me. I'm not the address."

Defense: "Yoram Rubin testified that he fell on Rabin, why don't we see that in the film?"

Kempler: "I'm not a video or camera expert. I'm not the address for questions like that."

The address, of course, is the technical department of the Shabak, where the film was altered during the time Kempler decided not to turn it over to the police or sell it. But this was not a skilled technical department. While the film was being edited and altered, Yigal Amir was filmed a second time, during his reconstruction of the murder a 13 days after the event. And this reconstruction at the crime scene deeply compromised the validity of the Kempler film.

The first error made was enormous and was pointed out to me later by a man, who claimed he was the first to report it to the press. In the reconstruction film, Amir shoots with his right hand, as numerous eye witnesses saw him do. But in the still of the Kempler film released initially exclusively to the newspaper, *Yediot Ahronot*, Amir is shooting with his left hand.

And that's not all. In the reconstruction film, Amir has bushy unshaped sideburns past the middle of his ear. The shooter in the Kempler photo still has squared sideburns at the top of his ear. Another person was superimposed over Yigal Amir for the still and there may be one possible reason why. The superimposed figure's arm looks longer, thus reducing the range of the shot, a necessity to be explained shortly. This is just one possibility. There are others, so far, less convincing. Nonetheless, for whatever reason, Amir's image was almost certainly removed from the Kempler film still and replaced by another.

But the reconstruction belied the Kempler film in other ways, as reluctantly testified to by Lieutenant Arieh Silberman, Amir's chief investigator, at the defendant's trial.

Defense: "Did you notice the differences between the video shown on Channel Two and the film of the reconstruction? Did you see the reconstruction film?"

Silberman: "I saw the reconstruction. It was of the same event in principle but there was an obvious difference. You can see the difference."

Defense: "You're responsible for the defendant's investigation. Why is there a difference between the reconstruction film and the video shown on Channel Two?"

Silberman: "To my eyes, the difference isn't significant. The defendant doesn't think so. He never brought it up. I wasn't at the reconstruction."

Defense: "Why is there a break where we don't hear part of the audio?"

Silberman: "I didn't make the film. It was handled by the technicians of several units. I'm responsible for investigating the defendant, not the film."

Defense (Amir now acts as his own attorney): "Is there a difference between the original film and what was shown on Channel Two?"

Silberman: "Could be."

Defense: "What's the most outstanding difference?"

Silberman: "The position of the prime minister."

Defense: "In the reconstruction, I go straight toward him."

Silberman: "True."

Defense: "And in the original video I took a roundabout route."

Silberman: "According to what I saw, you circled someone before getting behind Rabin."

Amir reconstructed his alleged crime wrongly according to the Kempler film. And he shot with the wrong hand according to the still of the Kempler film. If Amir's attorneys had bothered to press the issue, they might have been able to construct a plausible argument that he wasn't even at the scene of the crime, according to the Kempler film.

October 1996 saw the blatant inconsistencies between the official version of events surrounding the Rabin assassination and the truth finally clash publicly. Early in the month, *Maariv*'s weekend magazine published a revealing collection of testimony from several policemen and security agents on duty at the assassination scene that fueled suspicions of a conspiracy from many formerly skeptical readers. On October 18, the author of this piece was the victim of an eight-minute hatchet job on Israeli Television Channel Two's weekend magazine show that was shown again the next night. Despite the blatant attempt at character assassination, as *Yediot Ahronot* reported the Sunday following, the *Maariv* article succeeded in igniting renewed national interest in the possibility that Rabin's murder was not as officially reported.

The author's appearance on national TV introduced to the Israeli public for the first time proof that Rabin was shot in his car and not by Amir outside it. Even before the broadcast was finished, a phone threat arrived. The caller said, "Friend, you're going to leave the country. For you're own safety, you'd better leave the country." The same caller persisted for two days until I traced his phone number (he lived in Haifa) and complained to the police. Though the calls stopped, the police did not choose to recommend prosecution of the threatener.

The Channel Two news team was incredibly deceitful, telling me they wanted to point out the inconsistencies of the Shamgar Commission. In fact, their goal was to hush me through character assassination. Minutes after the report ended, three Labor Party politicians, including former Health Minister Ephraim Sneh, who knows far more than he is telling, condemned my work and the news team itself arranged to have my lectures with two organizations cancelled.

But, I learned, the media is not the people. I was congratulated for my work by people wherever I went. The effect of the TV report was to shock the public with a "radical," "extremist" and "inciteful" theory. Within six months, the theory was accepted by thousands of Israelis.

First the *Maariv* report. We begin with the issue of whether the alleged assassin, Yigal Amir's bullets were real or not. It is not denied by the Shamgar

Commission that "Blanks, blanks," was yelled by someone while Amir shot his weapon. The conclusion it reached is that Amir yelled it to confuse Rabin's bodyguards, a contention he denies. It turns out that more than just "Blanks, blanks" was shouted.

> S.G.: "Shabak Agent Under Command of Rabin's bodyguard Yoram Rubin: I heard very clearly, `They're not real, they're not real,' during the shooting."

> A.A.: "Personal Security Head of the Shabak: I heard one shot and someone shouting,`Not real, not real.' I can't say with certainty if it came from the shooter."

> Avi Yahav, Tel Aviv policeman: "The shooter yelled, `They're caps, nothing, caps.'"

None of the police or security men quoted by *Maariv* heard the famous `Srak, srak,' (blanks, blanks) shout. The scene they describe is of a number of people shouting different phrases. What united the shouters was their belief that blank bullets were being shot.

Within four months, I had acquired the protocols of Yigal Amir's trial as well as the police reports written on the night of the assassination. What they revealed was that a wide variety of shouts were heard including "They're caps," "They're dummy bullets," "It's a toy gun" and "Fake bullets." What follows is a sample of official testimony:

> Menachem Damti, Rabin's Driver: "I heard the shooter shout, `It's nothing.'"

> Agent Sh.: "A policeman shouted, `Calm down. They're blanks.'"

> Policeman Ephron Moshe: "People yelled `Blanks,' and `Fake bullets.'"

> Accused assassin Yigal Amir: "I shot and heard `They're blanks,' from someone at the back, right side of the car."

How many bullets were shot?

> From *Maariv*;
> A.H.: "Agent assigned to Yoram Rubin's staff: I heard one shot, followed by another."

> Police to A.A. (His name was later revealed as Adi Azoulai): "Are you certain you only heard one shot?"

> A.A.: "Absolutely certain."

> Avi Yahav: "I heard a number of shots. I'm not sure how many."

S.G.: "As I approached the car, I heard three shots."

From the trial and police records:

Yoram Rubin to the police investigator, Yoni Hirshorn at 01:25, November 5: "I heard three shots in a row."

Yoram Rubin at Amir's trial: "I heard one shot, a pause and then two more shots."

Shabak agent A.: "I heard a shot, a pause, then another shot. Two shots, not in a row...The sound of the shots was different."

Policeman Yisrael Gabai: "There were three shots. The first one was followed by a pause, then two more in a row."

Policeman Yamin Yitzhak: "There were three shots in a row."

Agent Sh.: "I heard three shots but they didn't sound like normal shots. A policeman told me they were blanks."

Agent Ayin: "I heard one shot and then people shouting, 'It wasn't real.' I was interrogated by the Shabak before the police and I told both I only heard one shot."

Yigal Amir: "I paused between the first and second shots."

Policeman Avi Yahav: "I've been to countless target practises and this shot didn't sound like a gunshot. If it was a shot, it was a dud."

Police Officer Moshe Ephron: "I heard two shots but maybe there could have been three. The wall at Gan Ha'ir may have amplified the sound...The shots didn't sound natural. If they were real shots, they should have sounded much louder."

Police Officer Shai Tiram: "They didn't sound like normal shots, more like a firecracker than a gunshot. They weren't loud enough to be gunshots...The first shot sounded very different than the next two."

Policeman Chanan Amram: "It didn't sound like a gunshot, too quiet for that...First there was a pop noise, followed by another two."

Policeman Yamin Yitzhak: "I heard three shots in a row."

Yoram Rubin: "The shots sounded real to me."

Police Officer Yossi Smadja to *Maariv* in July 1996: "I'll swear I heard five shots, two clear and three muffled."

One policeman after another testified that he heard blanks or something other than a real bullet being fired. This is ample expert witness testimony that Amir's bullet(s) was, in fact, not real. But how does one rationally explain the great variance in the number of shots heard? The Kempler film only shows Amir shooting once. A second shot is heard shortly after but is not seen because the filmmaker at that moment appears to have decided to film the floor of the balcony above the crime scene.

The inability of security and police personnel trained to testify in court to agree on the number of shots is puzzling but on one issue all agree; none thought Rabin was hurt.

From *Maariv*:

Y.S.: Shabak Head of Security for the Tel Aviv rally: "I heard Rabin was wounded only when I arrived at Ichilov Hospital some minutes later."

S.G.: "I didn't hear any cry of pain from the Prime Minister and didn't see any signs of blood whatsoever... It wasn't until some time after that I was told that Yoram Rubin was hurt."

Adi Azoulai: "Only after a number of inquiries as to whether Rabin was hurt, did I drive in shock to Ichilov."

From a police report on the night of the murder:

Agent Adi Azoulai: "I helped carry the prime minister into the car from the left. Yoram Rubin carried him from the right. We put him in the car and Rubin closed the door and the car left... I wasn't certain if Rabin was hurt, so I phoned Ichilov to find out."

None of the security or police personnel detected any sign that Rabin was hurt, a quite inexplicable fact when one considers that he was not merely hurt, but supposedly shot in the lung and spleen by two hollowpoint 9mm bullets. And a clip of Channel One's television coverage of the assassination night shows policemen searching the murder spot less than a half hour after the shooting. There is no blood on the pavement where Rabin fell. Not a drop. The "amateur" film of the assassination exonerates the witnesses. After the film shows the blast from Amir's gun, Rabin is not pushed forward by the impact of the bullet, nor does he show pain. Rather, he keeps on walking and turns his head quickly to his left.

Before examining the next issue of the *Maariv* article, let us skip to the report on my research on Channel Two. Despite the snow job, one of my points came across loud and clear and went a long way to keeping my name from being totally besmirched. I showed the assassination film and pointed out that as Rabin entered his car, the opposite side passenger door is slammed shut. I said the only way the door could be shut was if someone was inside the car shutting it. This would be in contradiction of the Shamgar report, which has Rabin and Rubin entering an empty back seat. No one known could have been in the car. The Kempler film shows both Rubin and Damti outside when the back door was slammed. Channel Two saved my dignity by saying the door was shut by the vibrations caused by Rabin's entrance.

Throughout the country, people opened their back car doors and started shaking their vehicles. Nothing could make their doors shut. Further, Rabin's door was armoured and weighed 100 pounds more than the average car door. Add to the fact that the open front door of Rabin's car did not shut with the back, nor is any shaking of the vehicle in evidence on the film, leaving one to believe that someone, perhaps the real murderer, was waiting for Rabin inside the car.

Six months later radio announcer, Razi Barkai, attempted to justify Channel Two's explanation. He claimed to have phoned Cadillac headquarters and their spokesman explained that Cadillac doors are equipped with a special safety feature which automatically closes them when sudden pressure is applied to the seats.

The explanation is unbelievable at face value, and it did not stand up to scrutiny. A famous photo of Rabin being lifted into his car destroyed the case for Barkai. The flash of this photo is recorded on the Kempler film after the door is well shut. Rabin was not in the car to press on the seat and shut the magic door. This same flash would destroy the veracity of Yoram Rubin's incredible testimony.

Here is the testimony of Yoram Rubin, Rabin's head of personal security. On November 8, 1995 he was quoted as saying in the *New York Times* that Rabin's last words to him in the car were that he was hurt but not seriously.

Let's look what he told the police on the night of the murder and later testified to the Shamgar Commission.

From *Maariv*;
Rubin to the Police from 1:07 AM, November 5, 1995: "I lifted the prime minister and pushed him into the car."

To the Shamgar Commission: "He (Rabin) helped me get up. That is to say, we worked together...We jumped, really jumped. I'm surprised, in retrospect, that a man his age could jump like that."

From the Amir trial protocols: "We were lying on the pavement together. I noticed a break in the shooting and said to myself, 'There's a defect in the weapon.' I grabbed him by his shoulders and shouted several times, 'Yitzhak, do you hear me, only me and no one else, goddammit?'"

Rubin testifies that Rabin helped him up and they jumped like athletes into the back seat. The Kempler film shows Rabin never jumped. Even worse for Rubin is his timing. Waiting for a break in the shooting, thinking there's a defect in the weapon, shouting several times over, "Yitzhak do you hear me, only me and no one else, goddamit," adds up to, at least and perhaps well over, 20 seconds. The time between the second shot heard on the Kempler film and the camera flash when we know Rubin is no longer atop Rabin is 4.6 seconds.

Perhaps the most confusing piece of testimony concerns the critical moments when he enters the car with Rabin. The assassination film shows the opposite back passenger door being closed from the inside and the other back door appears to be pushed closed from the outside. Yet Rubin testifies, "We fell onto the seat together and I slipped between the front and back seat. His legs and mine were dangling outside as I yelled to the driver, 'Get out of here.' He started driving and I lifted his (Rabin's) and my legs inside and closed the door. This all took 2-3 seconds."

In short, Rubin isn't saying one true word. But driver Menachem Damti also lied about his whereabouts at the time of the murder.

Maariv reports Damti's police testimony: "I heard a shot and the shooter yell, 'It's nothing, a blank.' As soon as I heard the shot, I sat myself in the driver's seat, ready to go."

The Kempler film reveals the lie. After the shot Damti stayed outside and is filmed, apparently, helping to lift Rabin into the car.

A most curious incident occurs on the way to Ichilov Hospital, normally less than a minute's drive from the supposed murder site. The trip took from 9:45 to just past 9:53. Damti was the most experienced driver in the country. He had been the driver of every Prime Minister since 1974. But on the way to Ichilov he "became confused" and got lost. So with a minute and a half driving time to go, Rabin's driver Menachem Damti picked up a policeman, Pinchas Terem, to help "direct" him to the hospital. Damti, who was a last minute replacement for Rabin's scheduled driver that night could not and did not get accidentally lost. The drive from Kings of Israel Square to Ichilov was straight and unhampered. Neither Shimon Peres's nor Leah Rabin's drivers

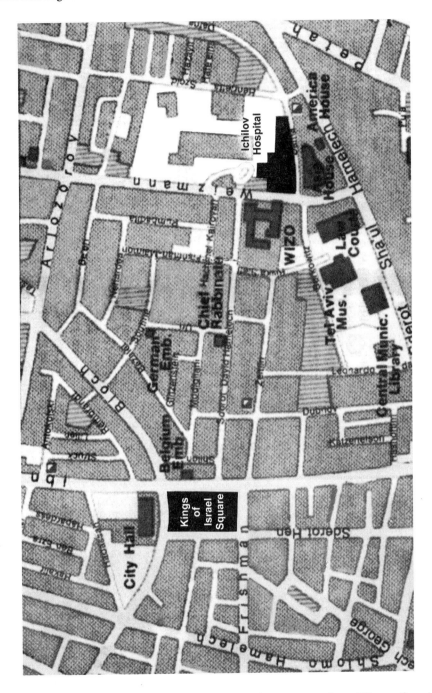

A street map of Tel Aviv clearly shows direct routes from Kings of Israel Square to Ichilov Hospital.

experienced any trouble speeding to their destinations. Damti took wrong turns though he knew the correct route to Ichiliov by rote. He didn't need Officer Terem's help to find the hospital.

Terem got in the car and with the Prime Minister dying beside him, the altruistic Yoram Rubin says to the new passenger, "I'm wounded. Bandage me." We can only guess he didn't care that Rabin's wounds needed much more urgent attention. Terem completed his bizarre testimony by noting that Damti did not notify Ichilov by radio that he was coming and thus the hospital staff was totally unprepared for Rabin's arrival.

Damti did not have to inform Ichilov by radio that he was coming. But someone in the Shabak certainly did. Damti had to lift the radio if he was really lost and inform someone that he didn't know where he was. Which he didn't do. When the hapless adventure finally ended at the gates of Ichilov Hospital, the security guard would not permit the Prime Minister's vehicle to enter. He registered the vehicle as arriving at just past 9:53 and Damti and Terem went scrambling out of the car looking for a stretcher and some help. Rabin entered the hospital eventually but no one, though reporters were there, ever saw or filmed him being admitted through the main outpatient clinic of Ichilov.

One conclusion of many that can be reached from the testimony of all the witnesses is that Rabin was unhurt by Amir's blank bullets and was shot inside the car. Rubin took a harmless arm wound to cover his role in the event and Damti picked up a policeman as a witness in case of future disbelief.

If this scenario or something more insidious is not to be given credence, all the contradictory testimony will have to properly sorted out by an honest commission of inquiry. And this hypothetical commission will have to answer how the back passenger door of Rabin's car really closed as he entered the vehicle.

LEAH RABIN'S
CONFUSING NIGHT

On 3/28/97 *Yediot Ahronot* published an excerpt from Leah Rabin's book about her husband Yitzhak's assassination. What follows is her version of the events of the fateful night of November, 4 1995, translated from the original Hebrew.

> "On the way to the rally, Yoram Rubin (Rabin's personal bodyguard) turned his head and in a threatening voice reported, 'Yitzhak, I want to inform you that we have a serious warning about the possibility of a suicide bomber tonight at the rally. Perhaps a terrorist will infiltrate the square tonight...'
> "At the rally, the wife of a *Haaretz* reporter asked me if Yitzhak was wearing a bulletpoof vest. Yitzhak would never wear a bulletproof vest on an occasion like this..."

Even when a serious possibility of a suicide bomber was reported to him by his personal bodyguard? What kind of a bodyguard would not insist that the prime minister wear a protective jacket, whether he liked it or not, in the face of such mortal danger?

> "We began to descend the steps, me one step behind him... Shimon Peres, I learned later, considered waiting for Yitzhak to exchange a few words but decided to do so at another opportunity. I was still on the steps while Yitzhak was already beside the car. The driver Damti waited beside his door in order to help him enter the car."

According to the Kempler film of the assassination, Peres waited for something but if it was for Rabin, he was standing on the wrong side of the car. As Peres waits opposite Rabin's car, there is a significant cut in the film. When it ends Damti is standing beside Peres talking to him; he is nowhere near the door Rabin is supposed to enter. Leah Rabin is so wrong on these points that it appears someone helped refresh her memory correctly.

> "I heard three blasts. Suddenly I stood alone and someone shouted, 'This wasn't real!' After that, a second bodyguard pushed me into the next car in line.
> "It was the same bodyguards' car that accompanied us from our home to the rally. The Cadillac already pulled away slowly with Yitzhak, the driver Damti and the bodyguard Yoram Rubin inside."

"The car I sat in then pulled away, past the crowds and into the street, not stopping for red lights. 'Where are we going?' I thought. I didn't see the Cadillac or any security vehicles. I didn't think the guys knew where they were going. Over and over I asked them, 'What happened?' and each time they answered me, 'It wasn't real.'

"'What wasn't real?' There was no answer. Were they just repeating what we all heard at the rally or things they were told through their earphones? The bodyguards were silent and obviously obeying orders given to them. I recalled Yitzhak being covered by bodyguards. There was a threat and they protected him. When I last stared at Yitzhak, before he disappeared under the bodyguards, he looked just fine..."

The last observation confirms that of numerous witnesses who saw Rabin survive the shot(s) without any sign of physical pain. The same observation is confirmed by the Kempler film which shows Rabin healthily walking forward after the first and only shot recorded on the film.

"According to our plans, we were supposed to go to a party in Tzahala. I realized we were travelling in the wrong direction. 'Why are we going this way?' I asked. 'It's the wrong way.' There was no answer. 'Where is Yitzhak?' the words popped out of me. 'If this wasn't real, Where is Yitzhak?' 'In the second car,' the bodyguards answered.

"'Where?' 'Behind us.' 'In what car?' I didn't see any car. 'In what car?' I asked again.

"Finally they told the truth. 'We don't know.'

"I asked myself why none of them tried to clear up matters by radio. This was very strange. Today I think they were ordered to maintain radio silence to prevent us being located.

"'Where are we going,' I asked. 'To Shabak headquarters,' I was told... I entered a modest room and was told to sit beside a table and wait. 'When we know something, we'll tell you,' said one of the Shabak agents.

"The moments passed slowly and I began to think the bullets might not have been blanks. Young Shabak personnel went in and out of the room.

"'What happened to him?' I asked ceaselessly. 'Don't worry,' I was told. 'When we know something, we'll tell you.'

"I'm not used to waiting but the personnel had no information. They did not treat me with friendliness or rudeness... Two sentences finally penetrated my ear: 'One hurt seriously, the other lightly.'

"'Where is he?' I asked. They finally admitted, 'At Ichilov.' It had already been twenty minutes since we arrived and if Yitzhak was seriously wounded, they would have told me. But they didn't say a word. 'Take me to Ichilov,' I demanded."

The story, needless to say, is bizarre. In what other political assassination, or mere murder, was the wife told repeatedly by different bodyguards that the shooting wasn't real? What kind of a reaction is that to an assassination? The only reason possible for the numerous assertions that the murder wasn't real was that the bodyguards were told that an exercise was going to take place; that a known threat was going to be caught redhanded after shooting a blank bullet. This is what the bodyguards thought had happened and this is what they hinted to Leah Rabin had actually happened.

Why was Leah Rabin separated from her husband on the steps and later trundled into a separate carful of bodyguards who seemed to be waiting for her and knew exactly where to take her, seconds after the shooting? How could orders to deliver her to Shabak headquarters be given so quickly? More to the point, why wasn't she taken to Ichilov Hospital to join her husband?

The answer is because she would have arrived before him. Rabin's car departed at 9:45 for the one minute trip to the hospital but arrived eight minutes later at 9:53. The reason given was that the crowd prevented a quick exit, something that did not bother Leah Rabin's driver, forcing Rabin's driver Menachem Damti to drive down back roads until he got lost. It would have looked most suspicious if Leah Rabin, who departed from the rally after her husband, arrived at the hospital well before him.

And how to explain the absolutely shabby treatment accorded the wife of the Prime Minister by the Shabak agents? Why did the bodyguards in the car lie to her about her husband's condition? Why did they ignore her legitimate inquiries? Why didn't they use the car radio to keep her informed? Why were they so dishonest with her at Shabak headquarters?

The answer is that orders were given to keep Leah Rabin away from the hospital for as long as possible. The last thing the conspirators wanted was a suspicious wife getting in the way.

AMIR DIDN'T SHOOT RABIN

Chief Lieutenant Baruch Gladstein's Testimony

Everyone who saw the "amateur" film of the assassination of Yitzhak Rabin witnessed the alleged murderer Yigal Amir shoot the Prime Minister from a good two feet behind. The Shamgar Commission determined that Amir first shot Rabin from about a 50 cm distance. Then bodyguard Yoram Rubin jumped on Rabin, pushing him to the ground. Amir was simultaneously accosted by two policemen who held both his arms. Yet somehow Amir managed to step forward and shoot downward, first hitting Rubin in the elbow and then Rabin in the waist again from about 50 cm distance.

The amateur film of the assassination disputes the whole conclusion. After the first shot, Rabin keeps walking, there is a cut in the film and Rabin re-appears standing all alone. Rubin did not jump on him and Amir has disappeared from the screen. He did not move closer nor get off two shots at the prone Rubin or Rabin.

And there is indisputable scientific proof to back what the camera recorded. What if the shots that killed Rabin were from point blank range and 25 cm distance? Obviously, if that were so, Amir couldn't have shot them.

Now consider the testimony of Chief Lieutenant Baruch Gladstein of Israel Police's Materials and Fibers Laboratory, given at the trial of Yigal Amir on January 28, 1996.

Gladstein: "I serve in the Israel Police Fibers and Materials Laboratory. I presented my professional findings in a summation registered as Report 39/T after being asked to test the clothing of Yitzhak Rabin and his bodyguard Yoram Rubin with the aim of determining the range of the shots.

"I would like to say a few words of explanation before presenting my findings. We reach our conclusions after testing materials microscopically, photographically and through sensitive chemical and technical procedures. After being shot, particles from the cartridge are expelled through the barrel. They include remains of burnt carbon, lead, copper and other metals...

"The greater the distance of the shot, the less the concentration of the particles and the more they are spread out. At point blank range, there is another phenomenon, a characteristic tearing of the clothing and abundance of gunpowder caused by the gases of the cartridge having nowhere to escape. Even if the shot is from two or three centimeters you won't see the tearing and abundance of gunpowder. These are evident only from point blank shots.

"To further estimate range, we shoot the same bullets, from the suspected weapon under the same circumstances. On 11/5/96, I received the prime minister's jacket, shirt and undershirt as well as the clothes of the bodyguard Yoram Rubin including his jacket, shirt and undershirt. In the upper section of the prime minister's jacket I found a bullet hole to the right of the seam, which according to my testing of the spread of gunpowder was caused by a shot from less than 25 cm range. The same conclusion was reached after testing the shirt and undershirt.

"The second bullet hole was found on the bottom left hand side of the jacket. It was characterized by a massed abundance of gunpowder, a large quantity of lead and a 6 cm tear, all the characteristics of a point blank shot."

The author rudely interrupts lest anyone miss the significance of the testimony. Chief Lieutenant Gladstein testifies that the gun which killed Rabin was shot first from less than 25 cm range and then the barrel was placed on his skin. In fact, according to a witness at the trial, Natan Gefen, Gladstein said 10 cm and this number was originally typed into the court protocols. The number 25 was later crudely written atop the original 10. If the assassination film is to be believed, Amir never had even close to a 25 cm or 10 cm shot at Rabin. As dramatic a conclusion as this is, Officer Gladstein isn't through. Far from it.

"As to the lower bullet hole, according to the powder and lead formations and the fact that a secondary hole was found atop the main entry hole, it is highly likely that the prime minister was shot while bending over. The angle was from above to below. I have photographs to illustrate my conclusions."

The court was now shown photographs of Rabin's clothing. We add, according to the Shamgar Commission findings, Rabin was shot first standing up and again while prone on the ground covered by Yoram Rubin's body. Nowhere else but in Gladstein's expert testimony is there so much as a hint that he was shot while in a bent-over position.

"After examining the bullet hole in the sleeve of Yoram Rubin, I determined that the presence of copper and lead, plus the collection of gunpowder

leads to the likelihood that he, too, was shot from near point blank range...
The presence of copper means the bullet used to shoot Rubin was different
from that found in the prime minister's clothing which was composed
entirely of lead. The bullet that was shot at Rubin was never found."

We now enter the realm of the bizarre, as is always the case when Yigal
Amir chooses to cross-examine a witness. Chief Lieutenant Gladstein has
provided the proof that Amir did not shoot the bullets that killed Rabin, yet
Amir is determined to undermine the testimony.

Amir: "According to your testimony, I placed the gun right on his back."

Gladstein: "You placed the gun on his back on the second shot and fired."

Amir: "And the first shot was from 50 cm?"

Gladstein: "Less than 20 cm."

Amir: "If one takes into account that there is more gunpowder from the
barrel, then the muzzle blast should also increase."

Gladstein: "To solve this problem, I shoot the same ammunition, and in
your case, from the same gun. I shot the Beretta 9mm weapon with
hollowpoint bullets into a jacket like the Prime Minister's."

Amir: "When I took the first shot, I saw a very unusual blast."

Amir is close to realizing finally that he shot a blank bullet but blows his
case when he concludes:

"We need a new expert because I didn't shoot from point blank range."

The Criminal Laboratory of Israel Police concluded that Rabin was shot
from less than 20 cm and point blank range, no matter what Amir says.
Furthermore, the bodyguard Yoram Rubin was shot by a different bullet than
that which felled Rabin or was found in Amir's clip. Unless Israel Police's
fibers expert is deliberately promoting far-right, conspiracy nut theories, Yigal
Amir's gun did not kill Yitzhak Rabin.

13
יג

KANGAROO
COURT

The most obvious starting point in the challenge to unravel the Rabin murder is to contact the convicted murderer's lawyers. However, Yigal Amir's attorneys were less than forthcoming. My calls to attorney Yonathan Goldberg went unanswered by him. Instead, his researcher, Mordechai Sones arrived at my home without any new information or revelations.

For a brief period after the trial, another of Amir's lawyers, Gabi Shahar was helpful. When Alon Eilat visited him in the Fall of 1996, he was rewarded with a copy of the brief to the Supreme Court submitted in July 1996 in which a witness testified that he heard an Ichilov Hospital pathologist tell him Rabin had three bullet holes in his body. This important document was released by Eilat in May 1997. According to Eilat, "Shahar was very helpful when I met him. After that he refused to accept my phone calls. I can't explain why his attitude changed so much but he just clammed up."

It's far from unlikely that he was told to clam up. In April 1997, I received a letter from a friend of attorney Goldberg, postmarked Tsfat, who informed me, "Mr. Goldberg was in the process of co-writing a book on the Rabin murder with an American intelligence writer when threats forced him to stop the project." Thus, the truth of what really happened at Amir's trial was never told publicly by the lawyers involved and seemed it never would be.

But on May 27, 1997, I was faxed a truly outstanding document. It was an interview with Gabi Shahar published just after Amir's trial in the Russian-language newspaper *Vesti*, translated into Hebrew. This obscure interview, at last, revealed the kangaroo court the attorneys faced.

Vesti: "You agreed to represent Amir despite the fact that one lawyer after another refused to be appointed on moral grounds."

Shahar: "I took on the case on 1/2/96, two days after Judge Edmund Levi asked me to handle the defense of Yigal Amir. My only condition was the defendant's consent, which I received. I was the third attorney appointed by the state and was given no preparatory material. I sat in my first court meeting without any preparation."

Vesti: "You took on a client who had confessed and was cooperating fully with the authorities. So what was the function of a defense?"

Shahar: "After reading the material in the file, I discovered many unanswered questions which the prosecution did not reply to satisfactorily.

"First of all, I noticed the following fact: In the prosecution's version, Yigal Amir shot three bullets from a Beretta 9mm gun. The first hit the prime minister's back. The expert from the Israel Police's Criminal Investigations Laboratory tested the prime minister's clothes and determined that the bullet came from 25 cm distance. In the video taken by Kempler, we all see the shot came from well over 50 cm distance. But let's talk about the third bullet. The tests show Rabin was shot in the lower portion of the back and the bullet's path was up/down. Yet, the police's ballistics expert testified that this bullet was shot from point blank. When I asked him about his findings in court, the expert testified that the bullet wasn't shot from even 2 or 3 cm distance— rather, point blank. But consider that after Rabin took the first bullet, he was felled and was already lying on the asphalt during the shooting of the third bullet. Amir, under no circumstances could have shot point blank."

Not one witness testified to the court that, after the first shot, Amir managed to get close enough to shoot another round from zero range. The opposite; everyone testified that immediately after the first shot policemen, bodyguards and Shabak agents pounced on Amir.

Logic dictates that the distance between Amir and Rabin widened considerably after the first shot. If so, a question: Why did the expert from the police determine the third shot was from point blank range? To my regret, no one answered this question.

Vesti: "Did the defense organize a pathological examination?"

Shahar: "No. Not one known expert agreed to conduct a pathological examination and the court turned down our request for funding to pay for the examination."

Shahar's revelation is astounding. No independent examination of Rabin's body was ever undertaken. There was no autopsy. The only proof of what happened to the body is found in the muddled and contradictory reports which emanated from Ichilov Hospital on the night of the murder. By the morning, Rabin's body was transferred from the privately-run Ichilov to the state-run Tel Hashomer Hospital.

Vesti: "In his files are other inconsistencies. For instance, the police ballistics expert testified that there were eight bullets left in Amir's clip. Another policeman testified that he had removed a ninth bullet from the chamber of Amir's gun."

Yigal Amir testified on numerous occasions that he had loaded nine bullets and eight were still in his gun. A question: who shot at least two more rounds? Perhaps Amir is lying.

Shahar: "What for? From the first moment, Amir has consistently stood on his guilt, revealing his act in great detail. On the night of the murder, his police interrogation was recorded on video tape. (*Vesti* interrupts to note that Israel's infamous police minister, Moshe Shahal, was also filmed in Amir's interrogation room, a fact that is probably very important.) Yigal Amir not only confessed to the act, he boasted that he fulfilled his criminal goal. He had no desire to lie or deny anything.

"As a former investigator with years of experience, I know how testimony is gathered in these cases. The interrogator must collect testimony with complete accuracy or it won't stand up in court. Already, during the first session, the investigator asked Yigal Amir, 'How many bullets were in the clip?' He replied, 'Nine, I'm not sure, but the clip wasn't full.'

"'How many shots did you fire?' asked the investigator. 'Three,' answered Amir. 'Where are the rest of the bullets?' asked the investigator in astonishment. He also understood from the beginning that there was a huge contradiction between the police report and what Amir was saying."

Police: "You originally said there were 9 bullets in your clip."

Amir: "True."

Police: "Does it hold 9 or 14?"

Amir: "The clip holds 13 bullets."

Police: "With the possibility of loading a 14th into the chamber?"

Amir: "No, actually, yes, yes. But I wouldn't have done that."

Police: "Then by simple calculation, we're missing a few bullets," observed the investigator. "Are you saying you arrived with nine bullets?"

Amir: "I didn't fill the clip."

If we believe Amir's testimony, after he shoots three times and a policeman removes one bullet from the gun, there should have been five bullets left in the clip not eight.

Vesti: "How many bullets can fit into the Beretta's clip?"

Shahar: "Thirteeen bullets in theory, but Amir was superstitious and according to his mystical theory which he presented to the court, if God wanted Rabin to die, two bullets were enough."

Vesti: "How did the judges respond to your line of reasoning?"

Shahar: "The judges called a halt to the proceedings immediately after they heard me. I had the feeling the judges couldn't answer my questions. The judges began a series of criticisms against me. Later when I presented the evidence of contradictions in the number of bullets from police files, they refused to hear my arguments."

Vesti: "Did you try and arrange independent ballistics tests?"

Shahar: "Of course. But the judges turned down our request claiming too much time had already been wasted on the investigation. Now my suspicions began to strengthen. In the files is the testimony of Shabak agent B.L., (Benny Lahav), who received a letter of warning from the Shamgar Commission that he was liable for prosecution. He demanded in no uncertain terms that the policeman who picked up Amir's gun hand it over to him. The demands were so intimidating that he contacted his superior, the head of the Yarkon police division, to protect him. What was so essential that this Shabak agent applied so much pressure on the police officer? I don't know to this day.

"Incidentally, there was a good opportunity to compare the ballistics reports in a different way; by examining the parameters of Yoram Rubin's wounds when he was in the hospital. This wasn't done by the prosecution or the defense."

In short, attorney Shahar suspects that Rabin and Rubin were shot by a gun that wasn't Amir's. The Shabak agent, actually head of VIP Protection Benny Lahav was desperate to get possession of Amir's gun before the police did. After it was in the Shabak's possession, the necessary replacement and adjustments could have been made. But the police kept the gun and their ballistics tests threw the Shabak's story to the wind. Amir shot blanks and only blanks with his gun. To hide this fact, the court refused to allow independent pathological and ballistics tests and no court pathologist examined bodyguard Yoram Rubin's alleged wounds to see if they matched Amir's gun. When Shahar insisted on expounding on the significance of the contradictory bullets testimony, the judges called a recess and later roundly condemned him for his "speculations." The kangaroo court was in full swing.

Shahar: "The prosecution took another route; instead of examining Rubin by an expert pathologist, they gathered suitable reports from Ichilov and passed them on to the court. But within one report by Dr. Hamo who treated Rubin, is his supposition that Rubin was shot twice. He wrote among other things, 'A bodyguard, about 30 years old, arrived at the hospital with two bullet wounds in his left arm.' I'm prepared to accept that one bullet caused two wounds but that has to be checked by an expert and it never was.

"Another inconsistency occurred when on his own volition, Yoram Rubin appeared before the court before the trial began and changed his testimony. He now testified, 'That it was said there were 4-5 bullets is wrong. I testify that there were three bullets shot.' But no one previously ever asked Rubin how many bullets were shot."

Vesti: "How do you explain Rubin's 'initiative?'"

Shahar: "As a former police investigator I'd say Rubin was terrified that he'd get the blame because he was responsible for Rabin's life. After I discovered this, I decided to question Rubin in indirect cross-examination."

Vesti: "What's the difference between direct cross-examination and indirect cross-examination?"

Shahar: "In direct cross-examination, I respond to questions posed by the prosecution. The prosecution, however, did not ask Rubin about the number of shots. But Rubin testified to a different number in his police investigation than to the court. In the course of the indirect cross-examination, I asked Rubin how many shots he heard. He avoided a direct answer. Finally, he said that while in hospital a friend told him there were four or five. As a legalist, I couldn't accept this explanation.

"In other words, the court claimed the following: Bullets were pulled out of Rabin, they matched Amir's gun, so why are you pursuing new evidence? But, let's look what happened to the bullets from the crime scene to the police laboratory. The pathologist Yehuda Hiss testified that the bullets were transferred to a safe in the Legal Medicine Institute. He doesn't testify who transferred them or when, even though both facts, according to the law, must be registered.

"The bullets were removed from the body of the deceased at about 2 AM at Ichilov Hospital. The Institute transferred them to the Crime Identification Laboratory of Central Police Headquarters at midnight the next evening. Who took the bullets to the police headquarters at Abu Kabir? Who delivered them to the Criminal Investigation laboratory? Talk about breaking the chain of evidence.

"In court I stressed that the prosecution had not proved that the bullets tested by the police laboratory were the same bullets removed from Rabin. The judge replied, 'Why are you bringing up this proof when the defendant has already stubbornly confessed that it was he who did the shooting?'

"In practice, the incident was like this: We accuse someone of drug sell-ing on the basis that a plastic bag of dope had his fingerprints on it. But the investigator did not register the bag as evidence so the accused is released for lack of evidence. In every legal hearing, once there are holes in the chain of evidence, all responsibility falls on the prosecution and not the defense. In this criminal case, most of the burden of proof fell on the defense.

"No one could account for the whereabouts of the bullets pulled out of Rabin's body for 11 hours. The chain of evidence was broken and one attorney told me that Amir's case would have been thrown out of most American courts. There was no legal physical evidence linking him to the crime.

"The bullets that the public was permitted to see in newspaper photos were in noticeably fine shape for hollowpoints that were supposed to ex-pand and shatter upon impact. To one police medic, the whole issue of hollow point bullets is illogical. She told me, 'Yigal Amir's brother Hagai was convicted of hollowing out the bullets. Why would he need to? Hollow points are legal in Israel and can be purchased as easily as regular bullets. Why hollow them out when Yigal Amir or his brother could have just bought them?'"

Vesti: "How did the court react to your line of questions?"

Shahar: "After presenting my assumptions about the internal contradic-tions within Amir's case, the court rejected them all."

Vesti: "What did you base your theory on?"

Shahar: "Simple. Yigal Amir was most energetic in his desire to be con-victed of the murder of the prime minister. Thus, he had no interest in lying or obfuscating to prove the opposite. The paradox is that during the hearing, Amir himself began to acquire doubts."

Vesti: "What were Yigal Amir's doubts?"

Shahar: "About a few things. He was genuinely shocked when, as he was shooting, someone yelled, 'They're not real. They're blank bullets.'"

Vesti: "And what happened in court?

(Before he answered the question, Shahar quoted a *Yediot Ahronot* report by Yael Horovitz, which read, "A group of people very near the Prime Minister heard the cries, 'Blanks, blanks.' A right wing source says he heard the cries from one of the bodyguards.')

Shahar: Now let's examine Amir's police interrogation as recorded by the court protocols.

> Investigator: *As far as I understand, you waited and prepared yourself for this?*
>
> Amir: *Don't know... I'll tell you there were strange things. Maybe you won't believe me, but to this day I didn't know I was going to kill Rabin. That is to say, I said to myself if there's an opportunity... I stood there and watched, I stood there among them for 50 minutes and no one said a thing.*
>
> Investigator: *What do you mean 'among them?' Among who?*
>
> Amir: *Among the police and bodyguards.*
>
> Investigator: *Among the police and bodyguards?*
>
> Amir: *There are things that are...(deleted from the protocols). They yelled, 'It's a blank.'*
>
> Investigator: *You don't think that was a screwup, that the guards didn't function correctly?*
>
> Amir: *What do you mean? 'Why did they have to shout 'It's a blank bullet?' Would a bodyguard watching the prime minister get shot really shout, 'They're blank bullets?'*
>
> Investigator: *That is strange.*

"The judge asked me, 'Are you implying that Amir didn't shoot Rabin? Then whose bullets did?' I answered him like this: 'Someone who knew ahead of time that blank bullets were being fired could have exploited the opportunity. He wouldn't have to be a government representative. Anyone who knew before hand that blanks were going to be fired could have wounded the prime minister with a silencer on his gun.'

"To my great sorrow, the court not only refused to consider the doubts raised by the defense but condemned us for implying that there could be any doubt."

Vesti: Did the court hear the testimony of Avishai Raviv, the Shabak agent codenamed Champagne? He befriended Amir and was held by the police briefly after the assassination, then released.

Shahar: No, Raviv didn't appear in court. On a number of occasions I tried to contact him to be a witness for Amir. With great difficulty I found his cellphone number but he pointedly refused to speak to me. Time after time someone else answered, calling himself a bodyguard or friend of Raviv's.

Vesti: Many have claimed that Raviv provoked Amir into action constantly. He was head of Eyal which publicized its existence on television. Wasn't the court obliged to have him testify and shed light on matters?

Shahar: All the police files against Raviv disappeared, over 15 of them. The one document revealing Raviv's criminal past that was presented to the court was done so in secret session.

Vesti: What was the general reaction to your defending Yigal Amir?

Shahar: Much milder than I would have guessed. Some people tried to talk me out of it but many others sent me faxes with theories and proofs of their own. For example, one woman wrote that the man who they said videoed the murder (Ronnie Kempler) wasn't the same man who appeared in court.

As wild as the woman's accusation sounds, the fact is that Kempler seemed to be a last minute replacement for another "filmmaker." When the amateur film was first announced, the name of the filmmaker released to the media was not Kempler, but rather a Polish tourist with a lengthy unpronounceable name, long forgotten. Someone thought the better of using him and instead, Ronnie Kempler got his fifteen minutes of fame...literally; he hasn't been heard from since.

Avishai Raviv, the most relevant witness of all, was not called to testify, nor apparently was Shahar given subpoena privileges to force him to be a witness for the defense, hostile or not. Without Raviv on the stand, the kangaroo court denied Amir any chance of a fair trial and prevented the Israeli public from hearing the truth about the murder of their prime minister.

Shahar describes a trial in which no evidence contrary to the established version of events could be presented, no counter scenarios vocalized, and no confusing testimony discussed. The court found no money or desire to organize the most basic pathological and ballistics tests. The fact that the evidence of the bullets was based on totally illegal procedures and baseless testing meant nothing to the judges. This was a show trial without any presumption of Amir's possible innocence. The idea was to give him a trial and prove to the nation and the world that there is justice in Israel.

But Shahar's description of the legal proceedings paints a very different portrait of justice in Israel. The trial, as he describes it, was as just and honest as the Shamgar Commission that preceded it, which means it was equally unjust and dishonest.

YORAM RUBIN, PANTS ON FIRE

The author is privy to an important document withheld from the media and public. It is the testimony of Yitzhak Rabin's personal bodyguard Yoram Rubin taken from the secret protocols of the trial of Yigal Amir, the alleged assassin of Rabin. As we recall, Rubin was the bodyguard who jumped on Rabin after Amir's alleged first shot and took his second shot in the arm.

What is surprising about the secret testimony is how mundane it is compared to what Rubin testified to in open court. That testimony is far more damning to his credibility.

The secret testimony begins with the court asking Rubin why the session should be closed. Rubin replied, "I don't mind being photographed but within my story I could touch on matters that I wouldn't want made public."

A representative of the intelligence services then explained that operating procedures and details of secret servicemen should not be publicized. The defense argued that the court could decide whether to procede after hearing its questions. The argument did not sway the judges and they decided to hold the session in camera and afterwards sign a declaration that they heard testimony denied the public.

The final declaration of the three judges Levi, Rothlevy and Mordick read that, "To prevent speculation, we must relate that the previous testimony was held behind closed doors, is not for public attention and will not be included in the trial protocols."

In one of the most bizarre episodes of the trial, Amir acted as his own attorney and personally questioned Rubin, one of the two men he allegedly shot.

Rubin first testified that seven bodyguards in two groups covered Rabin. He was then asked by Amir why Rabin didn't wear a bulletproof vest. He answered, "We judge the situation and decide if a bulletproof vest is called for. Vests are worn only in exceptional cases. The bodyguards never wear them." At this point Rubin makes a rather remarkable statement. "There were previous warnings that an incident could happen."

Needless to say, if there were prior warnings, then it was up to Rubin to make certain Rabin was wearing a bulletproof vest. Amir did not jump on this point, rather he returned to the question of the makeup of Rabin's bodyguard formation.

Amir: "You pointed out that seven bodyguards surrounded Rabin."

Rubin: "There were seven attached to him and twenty in all. I was the commander of one group, I walked beside him, another preceded him, another man walked behind him and he was joined by someone to the left, they formed the pair guarding the rear. One other proceeded forward and another right to cover the fence on Ibn Gvirol Street."

Amir: "You were with Rabin on the left side."

Rubin: "No. I didn't walk on his left."

Amir now questioned the security arrangements but did not make his point. Instead, he digressed, asking questions about whether bulletproof vests can be discerned under clothing. His attorney, Jonathan Goldberg addressed Rubin to help get Amir back on the right track.

Defense: "Was the protective ring around Rabin different at this rally than at other events because according to the defendant, he circled the Prime Minister and saw that his protective guard was different?"

Rubin: "It was different."

Defense: "The defendant says that at prior events the formation was two bodyguards on the side, one in front and another in back but this time the formation was different."

Amir: "At the rally when I got into Rabin's range, a hole opened up for me, I walked around someone and came in from the side. I always wanted to kill Rabin but I didn't believe that I'd ever have room to push my hand right to him. But that's what happened in this case. When I walked towards him I saw a gap open and I shot him in the back."

In this round he admits to murdering Rabin but has planted deep suspicions that he had help from Rubin and other Shabak agents. He stops just short of saying he couldn't have done it without their help. Of course, the judges didn't see it that way. But any other objective observer would ask why Rabin wasn't wearing a bulletproof vest if warnings against his life were received, why the bodyguards changed their regular formation that night and how did they allow the gap to open which permitted Amir an unhampered shot at the Prime Minister?

Now let's have a look at the testimony of Yoram Rubin to the police investigator Yoni Hirshorn on the night of the murder:

Rubin: "There were three shots in a row... I picked up Rabin and threw him in the car. I lay him on the seat and asked him if he was shot. He told me he thought so but not too badly... He lost consciousness and I quickly attempted to revive him..."

Compare this with his testimony at Amir's trial. Rubin was on the stand twice. We will begin with his testimony given on 1/29/96.

Rubin: "On 11/4/95, I was the Prime Minister's bodyguard. We descended the steps and for tactical reasons I moved half a step right toward the crowd thinking Yitzhak was going there to shake hands. Suddenly he changed his mind and walked left toward the car. In principle we were supposed to get in the far right back door but we never got there."

According to Rubin, it was Rabin himself who changed directions. That lets him off the hook for not spotting Amir nor covering Rabin in time. He was going right, while Rabin altered the route and turned left. Hence, he was out of position to protect Rabin just at the moment Amir shot. Rubin also begins his testimony with a plausible explanation of why the right back door was open...though he does not explain why it shut from the inside before he, the driver or Rabin were in the car.

Rubin: "As he turned left and we were opposite the back door on the driver's side, I heard a shot from 45 degrees behind me to the left. At this point I doubted that it was a gunshot. Then I realized, it was a shot. I grabbed Yitzhak and covered him. At this point we fell down. Now I felt a hit in my shoulder area like a jolt of electricity and I heard a third shot. We continued lying on the ground. I wish to stress the following points. I grabbed (Rabin) with both hands. As I lay on his back a bullet entered my elbow and exited the armpit... I have no doubt that there were three shots not four or five like it was said. There was a gap between the first and second shot. This gave me time to cover the Prime Minister. Then came two quick shots, one after another. I noticed there was a hiatus in the shooting and I thought to myself that there was a defect in the weapon or that the shooter was apprehended.

"I grabbed Rabin by the shoulders, I told him, 'Do you hear me, just me and no one else?' This I shouted. 'Goddamit, do you hear me?' I repeated several times. Then there was a period I don't recall and I found myself on top of him in the car. Damti drove us to Ichilov for medical treatment. The ride, I estimate took a minute and a half but I'm not sure. I was in the hospital for five days according to the newspapers. Now I'm alright."

Rubin stresses there were three shots not four or five though no one has testified to hearing that many. He says there was a gap between shots one and two though he told the police previously that the shots came in a row.

What he forgets is most fortuitous for him. He had previously testified to the Shamgar Commission that Rabin was alive after the shots. Not just alive:

"He helped me get up. Then we jumped. In retrospect I'm amazed that a man his age could jump like that...We jumped into the car, he on the seat, me between the seats. Both our legs were dangling outside. I put his in, then mine and told Damti to get moving."

How fortunate he did not repeat this nonsense again, since it didn't happen and since it contradicted his statement to the police that he tossed Rabin into the car.

The ride took a minute and a half? Not according to the driver or to Ichilov records. It took just over eight minutes. And fully conscious with a wound to the arm, he didn't remember how many days he was in the hospital? Instead, he relied on the newspapers to remind him.

Rubin: "I didn't see the defendant... I stood behind and to the right of the Prime Minister. To his left another person walked in front (of Amir). He wasn't the one they arrested, they arrested the one behind him."

Rubin didn't see Amir but he got a good look at a person walking to his left ahead of him. If he didn't see Amir, how did he know the other person was walking in front of him and to the left? And how could he tell which one was arrested?

Rubin: "I heard people saying the bullets were blanks. I don't know who said this. They said the gun was a fake or the bullets were blanks, I'm not sure which version is right and it doesn't interest me. I didn't think the bullets were blanks, I felt they weren't blanks. The first shot also didn't sound real. But you don't take chances."

Rubin testifies that the bullets sounded like blanks and implies that's why people shouted that they were. But he knew differently. This is a weak attempt to explain away the mystery of why so many other bodyguards thought the shooting was staged.

Defense: "Peres and Rabin descended the steps separately. Don't they usually descend together?"

Prosecution: "Objection. We know what happened."

Court: "Objection sustained."

Defense: "Was there a difference in the sound between the first bullet and the last two?"

Rubin: "Yes. After the first shot, I jumped on him and we fell together to the ground. I spoke to Yitzhak and we jumped into the car."

Defense: "Did you hear the shout of 'They're blanks' during the gap between the first and second shots?"

Rubin: "No, at the end."

We will never know why Rabin and Peres did not descend the steps together as was the custom, but we do know Rubin's testimony is unravelling.

Instead of the blank spot in his memory between the time of the shots and finding himself in the car, Rubin's memory returns and he recalls jumping into the car with Rabin; an event the Kempler film proves didn't happen and which contradicts his statement to the police that he tossed Rabin into the car. And the Kempler film shows that after the first shot, Rubin did not immediately jump on Rabin. Instead Rabin keeps walking. The film never shows Rubin felling Rabin. But his memory deeply fails him on another issue:

Just minutes before, he testified that he heard the "Blanks" shout after the first shot, now it's after the third.

Rubin's second round of testimony was on March 4, 1996. Until then, testimony of other witnesses put Rubin's version of events in deep jeopardy.

According to Rubin, he was lying on the ground atop Rabin when he was shot through the elbow and the bullet exited his armpit. Other Shabak officers and one policeman, Yisrael Gabai, testified that Amir was being held while standing and he shot his last two bullets downward at Rubin and Rabin. The defense pressed the issue:

How could a bullet shot from above travel horizontally from the elbow to the armpit? On March, 3 1996 Dr. Kluger explained that it couldn't.

Dr. Kluger: "You don't have to be a mathematician to understand that a bullet enters a body in a straight line. In order for a shot to enter at 45 degrees, as was the case in the second bullet, the shooter has to be lying down, not standing."

On March 4, 1996 Dr. Yehuda Hiss, the patholgist on duty at Ichilov Hospital, testified just before Rubin was to return to the stand. He said that Dr. Raviv (no apparent relation to Avishai) was the first to examine Rubin and he was apparently not overly concerned.

Dr. Hiss: "In this case, we are talking about a friction wound, that is to say, the bullet just grazed him. It did not penetrate the skin at all. We are talking about a superficial injury that caused a minor scrape."

So why, according to the newspapers, was Rubin hospitalized for five days? And why, to this day, does the Israeli public think the courageous Rubin took a serious wound in the arm?

Because another doctor, Yoram Hamo reported that: "There was a gunshot wound under the elbow. Under the armpit two entrance wounds were found." How can two doctors at the same hospital produce two such drastically different reports? Dr. Hiss has Rubin not shot at all, merely grazed, while Dr. Hamo originally concludes he was shot twice. Later, he claimed that the x-rays revealed two exit wounds in the armpit made by one bullet.

Something was very wrong about Rubin's account of how he was shot and he was in trouble when he sat down to testify after Hiss.

Defense: "On the same night, you testified to the police from the hospital."

Rubin: "That's true. I don't say things that aren't true."

Defense: "A gun was given to Damti (at the hospital). Was it yours?"

Rubin: "Yes. Damti was the departed Prime Minister's driver, bless his memory. I was afraid, I didn't know who was passing in the corridor. I feared that an Arab or some minority member would take my gun and I asked Damti to watch it for me. That's all."

How likely is it that Arabs were roaming around the corridor where the Prime Minister and his bodyguard were being treated? What other minorities was Rubin afraid of? In fact, the corridor was crawling with security personnel. Why did Rubin give his gun to Damti? More to the point, what did Damti need it for at that moment? Rubin's gun was not examined by the police and ceased being an issue at the trial.

Defense: "Before the rally, were you shown photos of suspects?"

Rubin: "I'm not interested in answering that." (The court requested that the witness write his answer on a piece of paper and submit it to the judges).

The only possible reason Rubin refused to answer was that he was shown a photo of Amir before the rally and the court didn't want anyone to know it.

Defense: "Tell us what happened after the first shot."

Rubin: "I grabbed Yitzhak as I previously explained, we began falling together, and as we were going down but not yet on the ground, I heard another shot. I identified the third shot while we were on the ground. I was hit with the second shot."

Rubin completely altered his story to fit the new evidence. Since medically and ballistically he could not have been shot while lying down, he changed his previous testimony to the court, police and Shamgar Commission. Now he was shot at the exact moment he began to fall. In other words, while almost standing. And how does he explain his about-face and the threat of being charged with perjury?

Rubin (to the court): "My previous testimony was taken an hour after the event while I was under tranquilizing medicine and in pain. If there are things that aren't exact..."

Defense: "You previously testified..." (testimony concerning bullet read).

Rubin: "Here, the version is mistaken. The real story is that I was in a bent position just beginning to fall."

Thus concludes the lying saga of Yoram Rubin. Everything he had previously testified to the court, police, and Shamgar Commission was false but the court thought that was okay because he was on tranquilizers in the hospital. The fact that he was not on tranquilizers at the Shamgar Commission or during his first session at the court and still lied meant nothing to the judges. The pursuit of truth was not the objective of this trial.

RUBIN'S MYSTERIOUS TRIPS

Tuesday, July 6, 1999 was supposed to be the first day of Shabak provocateur Avishai Raviv's trial for not preventing the murder of Yitzhak Rabin. The truthseekers of Israel were ready, and thanks to radio and newspaper articles by Adir Zik and Nadia Matar, hundreds were planning to attend as witnesses. So the plotters cancelled the trial and rescheduled it for September first, same place, Jerusalem Bet Mishpat (The Courthouse) Shalom, same time 8:30 AM.

This trial also was postponed, although it finally opened on February 22, 2000, in Jerusalem, behind closed doors—visitors and the press were excluded, with no protest. Almost no information about the trial or its discussions has been released to the public since then (as of May 1, 2000).

Every time those in charge of the coverup pull one of their stunts, I have released sensitive information that I had previously held back because I lacked the full story. In the summer of 1999, after Tel Aviv Police closed the complaint jointly signed by twenty citizens on March 10 to reexamine vital evidence and, essentially, reopen the Rabin murder investigation, I released the hint: Peres, France. I did not elaborate. A French Jewish journalist, Pierre Lurcat, published an accusation that Mitterand advised Peres about his own staged assassination plot early in his career and that Peres was more than merely fascinated by the details. The journalist noted that Shabak chief Carmi Gillon was in Paris the night of the assassination, he believed, receiving post-murder intelligence commands. The newspaper which printed the story came under such heavy attack that the journalist suspects he hit the scenario on the head.

Since I was missing complete documentation, I did not include this episode in the earlier edition of this book. However, I believe the French connection to Rabin's murder is real and if Carmi Gillon wishes that it weren't, he had better, once and for all, explain what he was doing in Paris on the night of Rabin's murder.*

---

*(Foot)Note: In Gillon's book, published in May, 2000, he confirms my charge; yes, he was meeting with French Intelligence figures, he claims, to discuss Algerian terrorism.

In the wake of these attempts to squelch inquiries into Raviv's role, I release the bizarre army and personal records of Yoram Rubin, Rabin's personal bodyguard, whose lies to the police, Shamgar Commission and the judges at Yigal Amir's trial I record in great detail in this book. By process of elimination of those who were in Rabin's car for his final journey, Rubin is considered the prime murder suspect by many of my readers.

I received Rubin's army records from a soldier and patriot. I can say no more. He explained, "I've never seen a military career like it. Nothing matches his later career as Rabin's personal bodyguard. Such a position requires an altruistic and courageous personality; someone trustworthy who is willing to put another person's life first for an average salary. Rubin's file describes someone else, whose life should have sent alarm bells ringing in the Shabak."

The Secret Israel Defense Forces File on Yoram Rubin

From 11/23/83 to 10/04/84, Yoram Rubin began his military career in a combat soldiers' course, eventually achieving the rank of Master Sergeant. Rabin's Bodyguard Unit consists of officers. Rubin could not have led it. No sergeant can give commands to officers, according to the structure of the Israeli military. On 4/24/85 he was made commander of a riflery squad, not a high ranking position, nonetheless a proud achievement.

Then on 4/24/86, he suddenly became a truck driver, a position he retained until after the Rabin assassination, when, on 3/26/97, he was reinstated as an infantryman. Taking a course in truck driving is not unusual for an infantryman but it is not the means of becoming head of the Prime Minister's guards.

This is part one of Rubin's career that doesn't make sense to my informant, as he explains: "No truck driver is going to become a prime minister's personal bodyguard. That doesn't ever happen, even in something like Rubin's case, where he had a lot of family pull in the security world. An infantry sergeant cum truck driver would never be considered for such a sensitive post."

Part two of Rubin's story feels far more sinister. From March 1994 to April 1995, while Rubin was in the Reserves, and Rabin's personal bodyguard in civilian life, he began taking unexplainable trips abroad. On 3/4/94 Rubin took a three day trip out of Israel, returning on the 6th. Then four days later, on the 10th, he took a two day trip, returning on the 12th. He took a four day trip from 8/22-26/94 and finally, from 3/14-16/95, he took a two day journey.

This was his last trip abroad until Rabin's assassination six months later. But after Rabin's death, the trips began again, as we shall see.

The informant asked me to do a bit of investigating for him. He noted, "Very few Israelis can afford the luxury of a two or three day trip, let alone two of them in a week. This is nearly out of the question for someone on a bodyguard's salary. I have discussed this with a few trusted friends and we came to the conclusion that as Rabin's bodyguard, he accompanied him on foreign trips. But we don't know this for a fact. We'd appreciate if you could find Rabin's itinerary for these dates. If Rabin was out of the country, fine, Rubin has an explanation. If not, he should be made to give one."

This bit of research was a piece of cake. While Rubin embarked on his first voyage, Rabin was testifying at the Shamgar Commission Inquiry into the Hebron massacre. During Rubin's second trip, Rabin was in Tel Aviv addressing the Histadrut convention. During the third Rubin trip, Rabin was in Jerusalem cancelling a planned meeting with the Meretz Caucus (a political party). And while Rubin was abroad for his fourth and final trip prior to the assassination, Rabin was giving a major speech to the Knesset (parliament), condemning Islamic terror in unbridled language.

Rubin took his mini-trips on business unrelated to guarding Rabin. On hearing my results, the informant said,

> "I thought so but I had to be sure. Whatever these trips were for, and they were not weekend vacations, why did they stop six months before the assassination and start again right after?
>
> "My colleagues tried to come up with any and every explanation. Maybe he had a gambling problem and took three day gambling junkets? If so, why did he kick his addiction for six months and start again? Why would the secret service employ a gambling junkie to guard the prime minister in the first place? Did he have a lover abroad? Why fly to her twice in a week instead of just staying a week? Nothing worked. These flights form an abnormal pattern for a bodyguard, in fact for nearly everyone. He obviously wasn't paying for them, so who was?"

And now part three of the mystery of Yoram Rubin's life: the Peres continuation. After the assassination, Rubin utterly lied to the Shamgar Commission of Inquiry into the Rabin assassination. He testified that after the first of Amir's shots, he pounced on Rabin. The amateur film of the event proves he did nothing of the kind. The same for his testimony that Rabin helped him get up and the two of them jumped into the limousine. Rubin blundered just as badly on his supposed wound. He insisted that Amir shot him from above and that the bullet travelled from the elbow to the armpit horizontally, a ballistic impossibility. But Shamgar accepted every one of his lies, thus providing the basis for the coverup of the Rabin assassination.

Undoubtedly the Shabak and its Secret Service division, were well aware of Rubin's lies: so why did they immediately assign him to be the new prime minister Shimon Peres' personal bodyguard? And why would Peres be insane enough to trust the bodyguard who bungled away the life of his predecessor? And why did Rubin's trips start again? He took his first in nine months, from the 5th to the 12th of January 1996, as the Shamgar Commission was preparing its deliberations. It was the first of 16 such journeys abroad from then until the IDF records stop on 5/28/98. The trips now were more frequent, 16 in two years and five months, and a bit longer, averaging 5-6 days in duration.

The informant notes, "Rubin had travel expenses rivalling the wealthiest businessmen in the country. Do you think it makes any sense for a civil servant in a sensitive security detail to be a jet-setter? I'll tell you what my people think: we believe he was receiving and depositing money for services rendered and for keeping quiet. And that's why we think Peres took him on as his personal bodyguard without hesitation. That's what we think."

Rubin's Hospital Record on the Night of the Assassination

Then in April, 2000, Dr. David Chen found a smoking gun.

Dr. David Chen is currently the most successful Rabin assassination researcher at work. Using his insider contacts and impressive initiative, he has uncovered stunning new evidence proving the conspiracy to murder Rabin. He has requested that the new evidence be gathered in one explosive package and then presented to the justice system. My response to his strategy was, "What justice system?" Dr. Chen has faith where mine has disappeared. He faxed me a document of such import that I could wait no longer to release it. I called Dr. Chen and expressed the view that events are out of control in Israel and every weapon must be released in a last ditch effort to save our nation. The report he sent me had the potential to short-circuit the government. He reluctantly accepted my logic.

I have in my possession the clinical hospital report on Yoram Rubin, Rabin's personal bodyguard and as my latest evidence proves, the prime suspect as his murderer. Recall that on the night of Rabin's assassination, Rubin was reported badly wounded in the arm trying to save Rabin. The new Prime Minister, Shimon Peres immediately appointed the courageous Rubin as his personal bodyguard.

Recall that Rubin testified under oath that a bullet entered his arm, "like an electrical charge," at the elbow and traversed the forearm until exiting at the armpit. The bullet was never found. Recall that the Shamgar Commission, and the judges at Yigal Amir's trial concluded that Rubin was wounded by a bullet which entered the arm at the elbow and exited at the armpit. These rulings were central to the government coverup of the murder, since they served the dual purpose of proving that a Shabak (General Security Services) officer did risk his life trying to save Rabin and of deflecting suspicion of murder from Rubin.

These conclusions were false. The public was lied to.

Surgery Dept. Elias Sorosky Medical Center

SUMMARY OF PATIENT

Name: Yoram Rubin

ID No.: 5959979

Address: Morgenthau 31, Jerusalem

Admittance level: Emergency

Admission Date: 11/4/95

Date of Birth: 1965

Telephone: 02 863489

Release Date: 11/10/95

Patient, aged 30, was transferred from Surgery G for continuation of treatment. He was previously transferred in emergency condition from ER.

Wound description: Gunshot wound to forearm from under the elbow, leaving two wounds in the upper forearm under the armpit, causing a slight swelling and sensitivity in upper forearm. Patient reported inability to straighten arm beyond 110 degrees because of the pain. Bruise in distensible region.

(Note: To imagine the wound, point your finger from under the elbow continuing at an angle toward the top the the underarm. There the fold in the skin will be hit twice by the passing of a bullet. Yes, passing of a bullet, because no bullet enters the flesh. This is a friction wound. Now imagine Rubin shooting a gun from under his elbow to under his armpit via the underside of the forearm and you'll see what happened. BC)

Treatment: The wound was cleaned with a toxoid in ER. Afterward, in our department, Polydine was applied locally along with antibiotics. The swelling was quickly reduced. The wounds in the arm were clean. The patient was released in good health with no fever.

Signed by Dr. Laslo Kalmanovitch

(Note: Rubin's "wounds" were washed and Polydine (an iodine-based cleanser) applied. The swelling disappeared and Rubin was released. That's it. Rubin's boo-boo was treated with soap and iodine and he was home free. BC)

Why did our government tell us Rabin's bodyguard was seriously wounded and why did he remain in hospital for 6 days? And why did our government's commission of inquiry rule that Rubin was actually wounded by a bullet IN his arm?

Further, Shamgar accepted that Rubin was shot while lying atop Rabin, by Amir who was shooting above him. No one shooting from above could have caused the horizontal friction wound described in this report. The only way Amir physically could have caused the wound is if he stood in front of Rubin and asked him to hold his arm out for him.

Perhaps some brave soul will make a police complaint against Rubin for falsifying his wounds. Maybe others will apply pressure on what remains of our legitimate government and media to finally explain Rubin's role in Rabin's murder.

THE "KILLER" SPEAKS

As far as anyone can tell, Yigal Amir is certain he murdered Yitzhak Rabin. Until May 1997, hints to the opposite were mostly withheld from the public. There were two exceptions. At his hearing in December 1995 Amir asked reporters why they didn't investigate the murder of Rabin's bodyguard (Yoav Kuriel). He continued, "The whole business has been a farce. The entire system is rotten. I will be forgiven when people know the whole story."

Amir never repeated this kind of telling behavior again publicly. Instead he returned to his previous smirking, grinning, laughing, incomprehensible demeanor. Behind closed doors, Amir was different. However, almost nothing revealing said to the authorities was released. A rare exception occurred in January 1996, when *Maariv* printed a statement to a police investigator from November 21, 1995.

Amir: "They're going to kill me in here."

Investigator: "Nonsense."

Amir: "You don't believe me, well I'm telling you it was a conspiracy. I didn't know I was going to kill Rabin."

Investigator: "What do you mean? You pulled the trigger, it's that simple."

Amir: "Then why didn't Raviv report me? He knew I was going to do it and he didn't stop me. And why didn't anyone shoot me to save Rabin?"

Amir, on numerous occasions said he didn't know he was going to kill Rabin. What did he mean by that? By the time the Shamgar Commission began its inquiry, he had a story ready to cover the question. He didn't know he was going to kill Rabin, he explained to the commission, he thought he was only going to paralyze him with a shot to the spine.

But he said much more to the Shamgar Commission that was hidden from the public. In May 1997, the weekly newspaper *Yerushalayim* published a three part series of Amir's testimony to the Shamgar Commission's investigators, Amir Zolty and Sigal Kogot. Since this was a complete unedited transcript, much of what Amir says is didactic and boring. Nonetheless, he reveals a great deal of important information that he never recounted in open court when it may have helped him.

We begin with an enormously important observation. Previously, this book compared the still photo of Amir from the Kempler film published by *Yediot Ahronot* with Amir's reconstruction of the shooting. The picture shows "Amir" shooting from the wrong hand and sporting the wrong haircut. If that wasn't proof enough that another person was superimposed over Amir, he provides the coup de grace.

Amir On The Kempler Film

Shamgar Investigators (SI): "In one of the segments you are filmed shoulder to shoulder with three policemen."

Amir: "I saw the picture in the newspaper. Very strange."

SI: "Do you recall what they said in this segment?"

Amir: "I want to see that tape, there are some really weird things in it."

SI: "What's weird?"

Amir: "I look weird in it, I don't know."

SI: "Really?"

Amir: "What I'm wearing, the shirt. It's not just that they colored it in, they colored it blue in the papers. That's nonsense. I have to see the tape."

SI: "A tricot shirt."

Amir: "You see that it was rolled up to here [halfway]. In the paper you don't see that."

SI: "And in the paper you are shooting from the left. But it wasn't that way."

Amir: "I shoot from the left hand?"

SI: "You have to see the tape."

Amir notes that his shirt was rolled up past his elbows, yet in the still of the Kempler film published in *Yediot Ahronot,* the shooter is wearing a long-sleeved shirt. As soon as I read this quote, I rewatched the Kempler film.

There was Amir either wearing a short sleeved shirt or as he claims, a long sleeved shirt rolled up. The conspirators botched another detail of the Kempler film stills.

And worse, the Shamgar Commission knew it but never entered the fact into the public records. Instead the commission curtly and quickly dismissed all evidence of a conspiracy. But it was the commission's investigators who pointed out the fact to Amir that he appeared in the film's still picture shooting with the wrong hand.

And what does Amir mean that his shirt was colored in? In the film he is wearing a distinct blue shirt. Is that wrong as well? Not likely, as we shall see. Amir seems to be saying that his shirt's color was altered or enhanced. However, someone else at the murder scene thought it was blue.

Who Was That Usher?

SI: "You spoke of someone in a beret who tried to remove you or something like that. We don't know who he is."

Amir: "Yes, he was some kind of usher. I don't exactly know what he was."

SI: "You said he wore a tricot shirt with a beret on its side."

Amir: "He stood there all the time. He was an older man."

SI: "And what is this that suddenly he said, 'Tell them to come to you?'"

Amir: "Just interesting."

SI: "Were there barriers up?"

Amir: "Not yet. They began tearing down barriers. They photographed me from the moment I arrived."

SI: "We don't see you arriving. We see you at a later stage on the potted plant."

Amir: "The potted plant was at the end, a minute or two before."

SI: "We see you five minutes before."

Amir: "Yes, that's the potted plant I sat on..."

SI: "Alright, now you're standing two meters from the scene. People are approaching you and you have to explain your presence. Did you say you were a chauffeur?"

Amir: "No, because they'd ask to see my license and things could get messy. I thought I'd just act innocent, say I wanted to see Rabin... I hung around the cops saying nothing. So if they said that everyone had to leave, they would think I belonged there... Shulamit Aloni arrived and the usher appeared, causing a small problem."

SI: "What did he do? What did he say?"

Amir: "He said (to unidentified security personnel), 'Did you block the back of the parking lot?' They answered no. So he announced over his radio that it should be barricaded there."

SI: "Who are you talking about, the usher in the beret you just showed us?"

Amir: "Yes, I think. I thought it was strange that he was a civilian ordering policemen around. But I thought he was an organizer of the demonstration. Then he sent a policeman to clear out the crowd. Another policeman and a driver were ordered to leave."

SI: "Did the bodyguard beside Rabin's car see you?"

Amir: "Yes, but he didn't point me out. He gazed at the crowd."

SI: "Were the barriers up?"

Amir: "There weren't any. There were lots of policemen and no one could get in. After the driver left, the usher came up to me and asked, 'Was he one of yours?,' meaning the policeman. Then I understood he bought my act."

SI: "Did he ask you about the driver?"

Amir: "I don't know. I don't like to lie so I said, 'I don't know him. He was here by the car all the time.' The usher made a round and came back to order another driver beside me out. Then a policeman came and escorted him away. He shouted, 'No, no. The one in the blue shirt.'"

SI: "To you?"

Amir: "Don't know but he pointed in an odd way, like this, he pointed a bit at someone. The policeman came back to me and asked, 'Where is your car?' I said, 'Here, here.' He said, 'Good' and left. I continued standing in the same spot."

Amir says he was photographed from the moment he arrived. But by whom? He appears in the Kempler film that was released publicly only for the last five minutes before the shooting. He managed to get into the sterile zone because no barriers were put up. Then an "usher" in civilian clothes cleared out everyone around Amir, including policemen and chauffeurs but left him in place. Obviously if this "usher" was clearing out all the other drivers, Amir should have been removed with them. One driver suspected

Amir of something and shouted to a policeman that he is the one who should be escorted out. Minutes before the assassination, all unauthorized personnel were removed from the killing zone except Amir by an "usher" of whom the Shamgar Commission investigators had no knowledge whatsoever.

Amir On Like-Minded Friends

> Amir: "I got to the demonstration and saw a friend from Likud youth on a bus. He told me that Itamar Ben Gvir wanted to kill Rabin tonight. 'You know about this, of course,' he said. 'I told the police about it.' I laughed. In recollection I can't figure this one out. But there were a lot of strange things...I walked to the stage but security was too tight so I walked towards the parking lot. I saw a friend of mine behind there. A real left winger from law school. So I walked around and entered from the other side and just as I arrived, they began removing people from there."

Admittedly, the left wing friend from school could have been in the murder zone quite by accident. Or, perhaps he was surveilling Amir. But the fact that Itamar Ben Gvir was there is more than merely significant. He was a highly publicized extremist, famous for stalking and harassing Rabin. A month before, the media reported that he left a note on the windshield of Rabin's car: "If I can get to his car, I can get to Rabin." He threatened to kill Rabin that night and the police were informed. Therefore, they must have been on high alert against the possibility of a religious Jew in his twenties shooting Rabin.

You would think... But Gvir and Amir were not the only young potential religious assassins.

Buried in the police records of the assassination night is the report of police officer Shlomo Eyal who wrote, "During the rally I spotted two young men in kipas (skullcaps) carrying bags who looked out of place. With the help of a uniformed policeman, I checked the bags and examined their IDs. One was named Noam Friedman. We let them go." The other out-of-place young man was not named.

Noam Friedman is another political murderer. In March 1997, it looked like Prime Minister Netanyahu was not going to convince his cabinet to support an Israeli withdrawal from Hebron. The cabinet was evenly divided on the issue and its fate lay with three fence sitters.

Then a soldier arrived in Hebron and started shooting up the marketplace in front of cameras from three international networks. He was apprehended after killing one Arab and wounding six. The Arabs were about to riot when the PLO's intelligence chief Jibril Rajoub arrived from Jericho twenty minutes later. After he calmed the situation down, all three wavering cabinet ministers chose to support withdrawal.

By the next day, it was obvious to many that there was much wrong with the scenario. Friedman was expelled from his Yeshiva a year before for "unstable behaviour" and was admitted to a government psychiatric hospital for six months. He was released and shortly after, decided to join the army.

The recruiting center was warned in a letter from Friedman's hometown, the city of Maaleh Adumim's social welfare department not to accept Friedman nor ever "place him in any position requiring a weapon." Yet despite his long stay in the hospital, his disturbing school record and a municipal warning, Friedman was drafted. After his attempted massacre, the IDF promised a full explanation of his inexplicable recruitment. It was never released.

Suspicions arose that the IDF deliberately recruited unstable young men for devious purposes. These suspicions were reinforced by the impossibility of Jibril Rajoub's appearance in Hebron. At the time, the city was in Israeli hands and Rajoub had no right to be in it without prior permission. So what was he doing there? He explained to the newspaper *Kol Ha'ir* that he heard about the shooting over the radio and immediately travelled to Hebron at 180 km/hr. And no one saw him do it. Even at this breakneck illegal speed, he could not have made the ninety minute trip in twenty minutes. In short, the Friedman shooting, like Amir's, also looked like a staged incident.

So what was this killer doing that night at Kings of Israel Square? As researcher Yechiel Mann observes, "He wasn't there to celebrate peace or to hear Aviv Gefen."

Amir On Arabs

Avishai Raviv's superiors, Agents Kalo and Barak testified to the Shamgar Commission that he reported only on Amir's violent intentions towards Arabs and not on his violent intention towards Rabin. Amir, they insisted, was a potential threat to Arabs. He tells a different story.

SI: "Did you organize against Arabs?"

Amir: "No, no. This is nonsense from the media."

SI: "This wasn't the media, rather what others said in their investigations."

Amir: "I said we have to protect settlements. But hurt Arabs? In wartime, yes but never kill them before, God forbid... I'm alright with the enemy."

Amir On Eyal

Yigal Amir was supposed to have been an active member of the extremist group, Eyal. That is the image of him spread by the Israeli media. This image went a long way to explaining his shooting of Rabin. But he doesn't agree with it.

> SI: "Did Kach or Eyal members come to your seminars?"
>
> Amir: "They came just one Sabbath but I threw them out. I really gave it to them. I can't stand their types, just don't publicize that fact."
>
> SI: "There were youths who came to Hebron on the Sabbath and over-turned market stalls."
>
> Amir: "Not with my group, never. Ask anyone. I didn't let anyone near them. Once, at Orient House some of them tried causing chaos but I gave it to them but good because I can't stand that kind of nonsense... I wasn't familiar with extremist groups... Don't believe me, but I'm not a radical."

Then what was he? Do moderates gladly accept the blame for murdering the prime minister? While Amir's claim of not harming Arabs is born out by ample testimony, his non-association with radical groups, especially Eyal, does not jibe with the facts. He may have been trying to protect people from arrest by association with him. Then again, consider his testimony regarding Avishai Raviv.

Amir on Raviv

> Amir: "I became acquainted with Avishai Raviv at university. He was nothing on campus. He would organize Sabbath events and people didn't come. I came because it was important for me to see the places. I didn't admire him for his organizing talents...He was on the fringes before he met me. Only through my seminars did he gain legitimacy. I didn't understand why he would destroy it all the time with his publicized swearing-in ceremonies and the like.
>
> "Now I understand a lot of things, many more things... After the Goldstein (massacre), Raviv moved to Kiryat Arba and everyone told me he worked for the Shabak. Despite the rising suspicions, I got to know him as a person and I was a bit opposed to it all... After Goldstein there were a lot of arrests and people suspected Raviv was behind them. So they told me not to befriend him. I answered that even if he is a Shabak agent, he's a human

being...Avishai Raviv helped me a lot. He brought me a cellphone, he brought me lots of things... I have friends who are spiritual pals, who I can talk to and Avishai was a friend like that. He's immature and does a lot of stupid things but he's a good guy and I appreciate his character. There are very positive sides to it. He would arrange visits to childrens' hospitals and old folks homes just to make everybody happy. I still believe in him. I know he has a good heart."

SI: "There were witnesses who saw you and Raviv discussing murdering Rabin with a group of Kahanists."

Amir: "It's true that Avishai Raviv also said that Rabin needed to be murdered but I wasn't sitting with this group."

SI: "Did you ever hear Avishai Raviv say that Rabin needed to be killed?"

Amir: "Yes, I heard that lots of times."

According to Amir, Raviv was a hapless organizer, on the fringes of university life until he came along and legitimized him. And all the while he was boosting Raviv's career, he knew he was a Shabak agent. Even so, he didn't mind Raviv supplying him with a cellphone and other goods because Raviv was basically good-hearted, even though he constantly expressed his view that Rabin had to be murdered.

What we have here is one inconsistent story. If Amir knew Raviv was a Shabak agent, he should have had nothing to do with him. His excuse that even spies are people doesn't remotely make sense... unless he had his own Shabak ties.

Amir On The Shabak

"In the past year I had exact information about Rabin's movements. I knew which rally he would appear at, where he was going, every place he went."

Amir: "They pressed the Shabak into service against the people. And what are they doing after the assassination? Repressing the people more. It's absurd. It wasn't their incitement that caused me to do what I did... The head of Shabak said a lone gunman would never murder Rabin. So he incited lone gunmen to try."

SI: "Where did you hear he said that?"

Amir: "It was around. People think Rabin was killed because the Shabak didn't interfere with the murder. I say they couldn't have stopped it."

A rather mixed message but after all the fluff is off the cake, Amir is saying the Shabak had nothing to do with the murder. He has chosen to forgive Raviv for being a Shabak agent and probably ratting on the people who came to his seminars and he has chosen to forgive the head of the Shabak who he claims indirectly incited him to murder Rabin. He is being too gracious about the intelligence apparatus which manipulated him into prison for life. He takes the same attitude with the previous intelligence agency he definitely worked directly for.

Amir on Riga, Latvia

SI: We want to hear about your emissarial work in the Soviet Union in '92. There are a thousand and one speculations about this period. What did you do there?

Amir: The Liaison Office isn't so secret anymore. Once it was secret. They wanted organizers for Zionist activities and Hebrew teachers, all kinds of things. They asked my army unit (the religious Yeshivat Hesder) to send people. Every two months, they would change staff and I went with my friend Avinoam Ezer. When we got there, they were working with 15 year olds, trying to convince them to immigrate. I thought this was all wrong, that it was smarter to target older students. So I went out in the street with a kipah on my head and found them. I was a real attraction, a Yemenite with a kipah and eventually gathered 100 students around me for social events. It was a huge success...

As far as anyone recalls, Amir was a shy, introverted boy in high school Yeshiva and far from a gregarious soldier. However, his personality changed drastically in Riga. It is most unlikely that on his own initiative he went out on the streets collecting students. Nativ was an intelligence branch, not a free school. Amir was given practical training in social organization and returned to Israel with a new character and perhaps a mission he didn't understand.

SI: Were there bodyguards there?

Amir: Now you're jumping ahead.

SI: We understand you went through a personal security course.

Amir: Nothing, not a thing. Just minor security training. What are you implying? We didn't have weaponry, just tear gas.

Nativ members are not known for their openness. Even after over forty years of existence, little is known of its operations. Amir, almost certainly was on some kind of intelligence mission in Riga, however minor. Back in Israel, he duplicated his successes in Latvia on the campus of Bar Ilan University. He became an attraction in Israel even before the murder. After that, he became a worldwide attraction. And all because of a shooting that continues to confuse him.

Amir On The Shooting

SI: "Try and recall exactly who said 'They're blanks' or what was said. Everyone says they heard something different. And try to recall if you said something."

Amir: "I didn't say a word. And I wouldn't have said anything because it might have warned them. It's absurd that I would have said anything."

SI: "Maybe immediately after to save yourself, for example?"

Amir: "No. The 'blanks' shout happened before I was pushed to the ground. It was during the shooting. It's difficult for a person to shoot and shout, you're concentrating so much."

SI: "In the army they shout 'Fire, fire,' while shooting."

Amir: "Only in dry runs. I didn't shout anything. I distinctly remember that someone on my right shouted it."

SI: "What were his exact words?"

Amir: "'It's a blank, it's not real.' I'm not sure of the exact words but that was the message."

SI: "Not something like, 'Cease fire?'"

Amir: "No, no. It was, 'It's a blank, it's not real.'"

SI: "How did the shots sound to you?"

Amir: "I'm not positive. I remember I shot, they pounced on me and I got off two more shots. I recall the first thing the police asked me on the ground was if I had shot a blank or not. I didn't answer but then I remembered someone shouting 'blank' while I was shooting. It stuck in my mind; 'What is he trying to do to, screw up my mind?' I don't know, it was very weird. It didn't make sense that a bodyguard at the moment they're shooting at his prime minister would ask if it was a blank. He would first count on the worst case. Unless he was expecting something else."

SI: "None of the bodyguards said it was him."

Amir: "Does it appear likely to you that he would admit it today? They'd finish him off."

Why is Amir so certain that if a bodyguard admitted to shouting, 'They're blanks,' he'd be killed? That's a rather harsh penalty for shouting two words.

Amir does know more than he is telling, probably a great deal more. But he is either too frightened, too threatened, too intimidated, too brainwashed, too drugged or too ignorant to say anything resembling the whole truth.

There was no reason for the Shabak to keep Amir locked up in solitary confinement for a month after the murder. He had already cooperated with the police and confessed. He should have seen his lawyer and family within days. But it was a month before the Shabak felt he was ready to speak to civilians. One can easily imagine the kinds of gruesome pressure applied on him to stick to one self-incriminating story.

But the investigators refused to give up. They wanted to solve the central mystery of the 'blanks' shout and ideally, they wanted Amir to confess to the shouting. The questioning continued during the next session.

SI: "You know we have witnesses who say you did the shouting."

Amir: "I've heard that but it's not true. It was someone to my right, one of the bodyguards. I'm not sure if it was the one in the black suit or the other one, but it was one of them. I was shocked. Instead of acting to help him, they shouted that the bullets were blanks. There very strange things going on there."

SI: "What strange things?"

Amir: "While I'm shooting, he shouts, 'They're blanks.' I don't remember if I heard it after the first shot or the second or third."

SI: "Some say it was the police who shouted it."

Amir: "Not the police. No, no. It was a bodyguard. When I heard the shout, I was shocked. What, didn't I check the bullets? A bodyguard when he hears a shot, he doesn't stop to ask if they're blanks. He may as well just go home for a nap if he does that. He has to take action."

The Shabak is trained to shoot an assassin in 0.8 seconds. It takes longer to shout, "They're blanks. They're not real." Had the bodyguards shot instead of shouted, Amir could not have fired the alleged two more rounds. He realizes that something is terribly wrong but stops well short of saying that perhaps, he did shoot a blank just like the bodyguard(s) said.

Someday, he might draw just that conclusion if he puts what happened after he "shot" Rabin in proper perspective.

Amir: "I aimed at his spinal cord, not at his heart, his spine... I wanted to paralyse him, not kill him. After the shot, I stopped shooting to see what kind of reaction, bodily reaction there was."

SI: "Was there any reaction?"

Amir: "Nothing, he continued standing in the same way. Then they jumped on me from the sides and I shot twice more. But I don't remember anything about those shots. I never even saw Rabin's back."

Amir aimed for the spine and shot Rabin in the back. But to his surprise, Rabin didn't even flinch. So he fired again while being pounced on from all sides. But he didn't see his quarry, couldn't take aim and doesn't know if he actually hit anyone.

Perhaps now he might understand why they shouted, "It's a blank. It's not real."

THE RIOT BACKFIRES:
WITNESSES EMERGE

On March 30, I was scheduled to speak at The Hebrew University for a lecture organized by the Association of Foreign Students, an official students' organization belonging to the campus student council. However two left-wing student groups, Meretz and the Labour Party-affiliated Ofek decided to sabotage the engagement. For days leading up to the lecture, they tore down advertising posters and leaked disinformation to the media that I was a member of organized crime, didn't live in Israel, was sponsored by radical organizations, and that I was a Holocaust denier. The final accusation was especially insulting: Years earlier I discovered that a third of my family was wiped out in the Holocaust.

When the night of the lecture arrived, the saboteurs were ready. I managed to slip into the lecture hall by the skin of my teeth. The rioters in purple Meretz tee shirts blocked my way but not too much. It was more important that an obscure Labor Party Knesset Member, Eitan Cabel attack me in front of the cameras.

After I was inside, the riot began in earnest. About 150 people came to see me. Their entrance was blocked violently by about five protesters of the fifty who were there. The two leaders were in their early thirties, not typical students. They "fought" with student security men but as the organizer of the lecture, Brian Bunn later informed me, "Most of the security men wore Meretz shirts under their uniforms. They were there to promote the riot not prevent it."

Had the police arrived after a plate glass window was smashed and people, including one 75 year old woman, were beaten, the staged riot could have been broken up in thirty seconds just by arresting the two instigators. But two campus security officers later informed me that the president of the university issued orders long before not to allow the audience into the lecture. And, according to numerous people who called the police, the university refused to allow their squad cars to enter the campus grounds.

Journalists, however, were permitted entrance, supposedly to record my humiliation. But that was not to be. I logically explained what I would have said, presented evidence, and a few of the reporters started listening. This was not what was intended. So two campus cops tried to put an end to it all by escorting me to a private meeting with a Knesset member who greeted me for the cameras. I refused to budge and the reporters took notes.

Though most of them wrote the expected disinformation, a few, including the usually gutless *Jerusalem Post*, were balanced. And others, including *Yerushalayim* and *Vesti* published lengthy, favorable articles. Undoubtedly to the dismay of those who planned this riot to shut me up, my television appearances were dignified.

The result was a significant victory for truth. The most profound result of the national publicity which erupted around me was that witnesses came out of hiding, at least partially. Their testimony has so far proven believable and far-reaching. Consider some of the evidence that emerged because of a misbegotten plot to delegitimize my work.

1. Previous to the riots, I was interviewed on radio. A listener called the station announcer and asked him to act as an intermediary with me on behalf of his friend. The friend helped construct the stage for the rally where Rabin was assassinated. The crew constructed the stand with the usual security requirements. Shabak agents ordered the crew to dismantle metal detectors placed to secure the backstage area. In short, he said, Amir or any other armed intruder, was allowed to enter the backstage area undetected. Would the friend meet with me? Maybe, if I promised that his identity would never be revealed. If I agreed, I could contact him through the radio announcer.

2. After the riots, my first data leak came from the north of the country. It concerned Yoram Rubin, Rabin's personal bodyguard. "I think this is very important," said the caller. "I know Yoram Rubin's family well. I've known Yoram since he was a baby in Acco. The family has a history that would have prevented Yoram from even joining the Shabak, let alone becoming the prime minister's closest bodyguard.

    "The father treated his sons like a Gestapo chieftain. He worked for the government and was very secretive about everything, especially his work. The sons grew up under his abnormal discipline. One son, Gershon cracked after the family moved to Karmiel twenty years ago. He got badly hooked on hard drugs and stabbed his girlfriend eleven times. He got a life sentence for murder and died in prison, supposedly a suicide. The murder was in all the papers and it won't be impossible to confirm.

    "So how does a guy like that become the Shabak's choice of guard for Rabin? Do you know the kind of psychological and background tests they do before they'll induct you? I do. Yoram would never have passed. Something is really wrong here."

3. S. lives on a moshav and had a scary experience just because he noticed something in the newspapers. He had saved the papers of early November 1995, as did many people for historical reasons. Included in the newspapers were the photos of Amir reconstructing the assassination. Just over a month later, the Kempler video of the murder was announced and the papers printed half page, photo stills of Amir at the moment of shooting taken from the film.

    S. accidentally compared the photos of Amir reconstructing the assassination, on the 16th of November, just two weeks after it occurred. He was astounded. While reconstructing the murder, Amir shot the weapon with his right hand. Not surprising since he is right-handed. But in the Kempler film stills, "Amir" shoots with his left hand extended. And there is absolutely no mistaking it.

    And there was more. Amir during the reconstruction had unkempt, bushy sideburns to the middle of his ears. The "Amir" of the Kempler film stills had squared sideburns stopping near the top of his ear. Deeply disturbed, he took the photos to two Jerusalem newspapers. They confirmed his suspicions and more. The possibility of one photo being a reversed negative was eliminated. A reverse view would not alter the position of the shooting arm, it would still be left handed. Further, the profile of Amir without earlocks does not resemble Amir's side view in other photos.

    The newspaper editors would not publish the photos and warned him about showing them to anyone else. This was followed by threatening anonymous phone calls to his home. The information proved accurate. In the near future I discovered the stills were tampered with in other ways and that the Shamgar Commission knew about the tampering.

    Anyone who so desires may retrieve these photos from the archives of Israel's newspapers. The evidence cannot be hidden nor can its conclusion: Someone else's picture was superimposed over that of Amir.

4. I was informed tersely and succinctly that Yoav Kuriel didn't commit suicide. Kuriel was the suspected Shabak agent who died not long after Rabin. The cause of death was ruled suicide. His vital organs were removed from his body and he was buried in a closed funeral. Traffic at Hayarkon Junction was detoured for 90 minutes while the funeral took

place. This was quite an honor for an unknown suicide victim and it led to numerous reporters trying their hand at connecting his death to the Rabin assassination, but all in vain.

In his last moment of defiance, Amir shouted to reporters covering his hearing, "Why don't you write about the bodyguard they killed...The whole thing is rotten. If I said what I knew, the system would collapse. I didn't think they'd start killing people." After that outbreak—or more to the point, after returning to closed Shabak rooms—Amir turned forever more into a model witness.

Maariv reporter David Ronen managed to acquire Kuriel's hospital death certificate. In an illegal exception, the cause of death is not listed on the document. Ronen also found his grave in a lonely corner of Hayarkon cemetary. His name is almost impossible to read. It is nearly an unmarked grave, hardly a hallmark of Jewish tradition.

The informant told me, "I saw Yoav Kuriel's body. I wasn't the only one. It had six or seven bullet holes in the chest. That's not how people commit suicide." He told me we might meet in the future. But he never called back.

Not a week later, Ronnie Schwartz called me from Kfar Saba. He told me a friend of the gravedigger who buried Kuriel told him that Kuriel had seven bullet holes in his chest. He added that he had a witness.

I met Schwartz and the witness, Avi Shekel, in Tel Aviv. Both men were established and well respected businessmen. Shekel repeated the same story of the seven bullet holes in the chest and promised me that he would try to arrange a personal meeting between me and the gravedigger.

The meeting, it turned out, would have to be arranged by a close friend of the gravedigger's, Yehoshua Mittleman, who lived in the orthodox city of Bnei Brak. Without adding unnecessary details, the intermediary informed me that yes, his friend handled Kuriel's body and not only were there seven bullet holes in the chest but other vital organs had been insulted. The gravedigger, I was told, "Is not a Zionist and he won't risk his life for the country. He saw what happens if you get the wrong people angry."

On May 17, I was given Yoav Kuriel's social security file. I called Ronen and he came to my home to examine it. "There it is," he said after a quick perusal. "He was employed by Israel Police at Sheikh Jarrah Headquarters. That's where the police intelligence branch is located."

Kuriel's was not the only suspicious "suicide" connected to the assassination. An American student at Bar Ilan University, D.S., also supposedly killed himself because he was "depressed" about Rabin's death. A friend of his informed me, "He was close with Avishai Raviv. None of his friends bought the suicide story. He was shut up permanently."

5. Professor Arieh Rosen-Tzvi was the Tel Aviv University law professor who was a member of the Shamgar Commission. He died of cancer not long after the commission's findings were released. I received a phone call from someone who knew him. The caller said he had important information but he could not repeat it over the phone. The next day we met at my home.

The informant holds a most respected position in the educational field. He said, "I saw Arieh the week he died. He told me he was keeping deep secrets in his heart about Rabin and could never reveal them. A few days later he was dead. Cancer isn't a heart attack. You are bedridden in the final stages. He couldn't have died overnight from it."

The story was eerily reminiscent of another death connected to Rabin. At 8:45 on a warm, July morning in 1995, Rabin's deputy defense minister Motta Gur was found dead in his home. He had shot himself through the neck and had supposedly left a one line note saying he didn't want his family to suffer from his pain anymore. The note was never shown publicly. By 5:00 that evening, in unseemly haste, General Gur, the liberator of Jerusalem and a national hero was buried. The reason given by the media for the suicide was Gur's depression over his terminal cancer.

Just a few weeks before, Gur caused an uproar in the Knesset when, according to *Maariv* 6/15/95, "It's not that Gur did not merely condemn the settlers, he came to their defense. 'I must say I asked myself why we didn't settle the place years ago? In 1946, as youths, we founded thirteen kibbutzim the same way.' Gur's pronouncement led to hours of vigorous debate which almost resulted in several MKs being ejected from the forum."

Gur was opposing Rabin's "peace" process actively. He had recently visited Hebron and the nearby settlement of Barkai to encourage the settler movement. The settlers, in return, considered him their only friend left in Rabin's cabinet. And as Rabin's deputy in the Defense Ministry, he was privy to the kind of secrets those opposed to the "peace" process might find most useful.

But terminal cancer led to Gur taking his own life. Or did it? Not according to Gur's physician and the head of Ichilov Hospital's Oncology Department where he was being treated, Prof. Samario Chaitchik, who told *Maariv*, "Two months ago we found a brain tumor. It was treated at

Memorial Hospital in Manhattan. Seven weeks ago, Gur returned to Israel. He was greatly improved and his tumor completely disappeared, as did the side effects of his treatment. We saw him three days ago and he showed no signs of depression. He made an appointment to see us in ten days."

So much for the official version of Gur's suicide. His cancer was in remission and he had every reason to live. The night before his death he made another appointment, this time to be interviewed by television reporter Avi Bettleheim. Family and friends all expressed utter surprise at the death because Gur was not the suicidal kind.

I was immediately suspicious. How could he make appointments and plan suicide at the same time, I thought? Especially if there was no reason for the suicide in the first place. And who kills himself with a shot through the neck? And why was he, a cabinet member, buried within eight hours, before a proper funeral could be arranged?

Like Rosen-Tzvi's cancer, Gur's was seemingly an excuse used by the murderers to cover their tracks... just five months before his boss, Yitzhak Rabin, was assassinated.

ANOTHER
RESEARCHER AT LAST

In October 1996, television Channel Two broadcast a report about people who deny the official version of the Rabin assassination. Though, the program was mostly devoted to my research, a few seconds were given to a researcher from Ramat Gan, Natan Gefen. After seeing the program, a local reporter visited Gefen. In early November, the Ramat Gan newspaper *Hamekomon* published a courageous interview with Gefen, who had been researching the coverup of the Rabin murder for the past year. According to the article, "Gefen sat in most of the court discussions connected to the murder, met with numerous experts and is certain Yigal Amir had a partner in the murder...who is walking free." After a year of lonely investigation, I discovered, to my great delight, that I was not alone.

What follows are selections from the three page interview. I add that Gefen disagrees with my conclusion that Yigal Amir shot one blank bullet and that Rabin was actually murdered in his car on the way to Ichilov Hospital.

However, we were in agreement about details of the Shabak coverup, which I will comment on at the conclusion of his interview.

Ramat Gan *Hamekoman* (RGH): "Natan Gefen, what is your thesis based on?"

Gefen: "It's based on an accumulation of facts I read, collected and researched. Yigal Amir claimed in his first interrogation that he hadn't intended to kill Rabin, just wound him. Yet he shot hollow-point bullets which do much more bodily harm than regular bullets. So he must have been lying.

"However, hollowpoint bullets have much less penetrating power and he must have been given advance information that Rabin wouldn't be wearing a bulletproof vest. My conclusion is that he had inside information. Also, hollowpoint bullets shatter and cannot be identified once they enter the body."

RGH: "These aren't serious claims. Yigal Amir was caught, he shot three times and even reconstructed the event."

Gefen: "Yigal Amir shot just once and then was pounced on by Rabin's bodyguards. The next shot was point blank at Rabin and Amir never got that close. Amir never touched Rabin physically."

RGH: "How do you know that?"

Gefen: "From the film of the assassination and according to testimony given by police and Shabak officers."

RGH: "Yet, in his reconstruction, Amir shot three times."

Gefen: "His reconstruction wasn't accurate. He claimed that after he was held down by the security men, he got off two more shots. I don't believe him.

"After his gun was taken, the police and Shabak found eight bullets within. Amir claimed he loaded nine. Amir is hiding the facts."

RGH: "Let's say you're right, then who shot the other bullets?"

Gefen: "The answer was smothered previously. I insist that Rabin's bodyguards had to have been arrested on the spot. We're talking about the murder of a prime minister not a break-in. The moment they weren't arrested, they could coordinate their testimony and leave the killer's identity in the hands of the Shabak."

RGH: "So you claim that someone from the Shabak shot Rabin?"

Gefen: "Perhaps, or someone connected to the Shabak or maybe not."

RGH: "In short, you are claiming there was a Shabak conspiracy?"

Gefen: "No. This was a conspiracy between Amir and a Shabak agent who succeeded in gaining the trust of Rabin's bodyguards who aided in the murder. In my opinion, someone took advantage of the pileup on Amir to shoot Rabin."

RGH: "And who shot the bodyguard Yoram Rubin?"

Gefen: "I think it was staged because a third bullet was never found. The police criminal investigations laboratory found that the chemical composition of (Rubin's) bullet hole was different from the rest of Amir's bullets."

RGH: "Amir was interrogated so often, yet you say none of the interrogaters succeeded in getting him to identify his partner in crime?"

Gefen: "I claim the Shabak ordered him not to reveal anything because the damage it would cause would be greater."

RGH: "What interest did Amir have in agreeing?"

Gefen: "Perhaps they promised him an early release. Amir cooperated fully with the police, confessed and should have been permitted to see an attorney or visitors after a week. But Amir was held for over a month without seeing an outsider. Why? In my opinion, the time was needed to persuade him not to expose a partner connected to the Shabak."

RGH: "When did you come to the conclusion that Amir had a partner?"

Gefen: "Right at the beginning of the events. After the murder, the Shabak acted most peculiarly. Usually, people under investigation try to hide their involvement. That's how the Shabak acted after the Bus 300 incident and the IDF during the Agranat Commission. The speed with which the Shabak took responsibility upon itself and initiated its own inquiry indicates they wanted to short-circuit an even bigger scandal. At the Shamar Commission, the Shabak tried to prove that they screwed up and that's unnatural. I felt there was something very wrong and I appealed to the State Comptroller and Attorney General to reopen the whole investigation. Neither answered me."

RGH: "It seems more than a coincidence that your work appeared on television on the anniversary of the murder."

Gefen: "I sought out the media because I knew someone could rub me out. So I sent faxes and letters to as many people as I could so I'd become too known to kill."

RGH: "Don't you think your work hurts too many people?"

Gefen: "And the fact that because of Shabak pressure on Amir a murderer is loose, doesn't? I want to explode the whole matter. There's no telling what the murderer could do if he isn't caught. And if he isn't caught, it is an invitation for the security services to try something again."

I concluded that Gefen obviously had not seen the film of Rabin's back car door closing before he entered the vehicle. If he had, I'm sure he would have concluded that Rabin was shot in the car and not during the confusion of Amir's apprehension. We did agree that someone else shot Rabin and that the Rubin shooting was a red herring. However, based on the same assassination film that clearly shows Rabin unhurt after Amir's shot, I maintained that Amir shot a blank bullet. And though he intended to shoot Rabin, and that makes him guilty of attempted murder, the real dirty work was carried out by someone else.

Those details aside, Gefen's research appeared serious and there was no doubting his bravery or ethical convictions. He deserved the appreciation of all honest Israelis. But I chose not to contact him, believing from the interview that he did not possess any evidence that I did not have.

In late March 1997, Gefen read that I was to speak about the assassination at The Hebrew University. He called me and we agreed to meet before the lecture. Good to his word, he arrived and was one of the few visitors who managed to dodge violent protesters and get into the lecture hall. However, there was no time to exchange information. That occurred the day after the lecture/riots when he, clearly impressed by the volume of national publicity left in the wake of the incident, insisted we meet. He said he had the smoking gun.

I wasn't sure what he meant but immediately understood the significance of the document he pulled out of his file cabinet. It was the initial surgeon's report on Rabin from Ichilov Hospital written just before the coverup began and it reported that Rabin was shot in the chest from the front by a bullet which finally shattered his spine.

This was a smoking gun, though there are others. I was impressed with this discovery and his diligence. When the editor and a reporter from the Russian-language newspaper *Vesti* interviewed me after The Hebrew University staged riot, I recommended that they meet with Gefen. They did so and decided that a joint interview with me would make a fine, and very long article. The following is Gefen's interview for the piece, published in May 1997.

Vesti: "When did you begin your investigation of the Rabin murder?"

Gefen: "On the very night of the assassination I thought it was incredible that the murderer had such an easy time of it. I couldn't understand why Rabin's bodyguards let him down, so as a first step, I decided to record the television coverage of the assassination night. Other questions quickly followed."

Vesti: "Such as?"

Gefen: "Why did Rabin's wife arrive so late at the hospital? Why wasn't the hospital prepared for Rabin in light of the fact that his car had a mobile radio in it? Where was Rabin's car for so long if it only takes two minutes to drive to Ichilov?"

Vesti: "The Shamgar Commission found no wrongdoing, just negligence, by the bodyguards and the lawyers allowed to see the secret sections of its findings say they reveal nothing but security procedures."

Gefen: "Let me ask you a question. Why was the first investigation of the assassination undertaken by Shabak officials? They shouldn't have been investigating, they should have been investigated. And why didn't anybody charged with getting to the truth at least investigate the issue of whether

Amir acted alone or not and if not, who was behind him? My duty is to ask questions, not necessarily to answer them. Do you have any answers?"

Vesti: "No. Do you? What are your conclusions?"

Gefen: "Yigal Amir didn't act alone. The fatal shot came from a second person and it was through the chest, while Amir shot at the back. The real murderer is walking free. The judges at Amir's trial concluded that Rabin was shot twice. I say he was shot three times, the fatal shot coming from the front."

On the night of the murder, Health Minister Ephraim Sneh and Ichilov Hospital's director Gabi Barabash both announced that Rabin was shot in the chest from the front and that he suffered a spinal injury. Both men are doctors who were in the operating room and saw Rabin's body. It's not possible they were mistaken.

Vesti: "Where is the bullet that shot Yoram Rubin?"

Gefen: "I am convinced Rubin's wound was staged. The bullet was never found and the police materials expert, Baruch Gladstein testified that the bullet which made the hole in his clothing was of a different metallic composition than was found in Amir's other bullets. He also concluded that one bullet which passed through Rabin's clothing was shot point blank. If you look at the Kempler film, you see that Amir had no possibility of shooting point blank."

Vesti: "The film is of such poor quality that you can barely make out details."

Gefen: "Come, let's look at the film. I'll show you, in slow motion, how it was doctored. Pay attention to Rabin's reaction after being shot. There are 24 frames per second and if you count frames you can accurately time events.

"Notice Rabin is shot and then turns his head toward the gunshot. Do you know how long it takes the average healthy person to physically react to shock or pain; .75 seconds or 18 frames. And Rabin was no James Bond, he was 72 and in terrible shape. How long did it take Rabin to react, count the frames, 0.2 seconds. More than half a second was chopped from this part of the film. Now examine the surgeon's report. It reports that Rabin was shot through the chest and spine. Dr. Barabash reports on television soon after that Rabin was given two units of blood. That means he was bleeding profusely. So where was it? No blood was found on the pavement where he was supposedly shot."

Gefen understated his case. When I later read the full surgeon's report, I discovered that, according to Dr. Gutman, Rabin was given eight units of blood. Either way, he bleeding far more prusely than Gefen imagined at the time.

Vesti: "I don't see anything strange about that. The onset of bleeding can be delayed. The bleeding must have been profuse after he was put in the car."

Gefen: "Not so. When a person is shot fatally, he is lain on the ground and covered with a blanket to prevent more blood loss. There was no way there would be no blood on the pavement. None showed up in the car."

That is, for all we know. Rabin's car was apparently, not examined after the assassination. Not once in the Shamgar findings or the protocols of the Amir trial is there mention of an examination of the car, or its back seat. This was no simple oversight. I am certain someone in the police must have tested the back seat and whoever he is, he was never called to testify, nor did he volunteer to do so.

Vesti: "Who gave you the surgeon's report?"

Gefen: "Last November the local Ramat Gan newspaper did a story about my research. I copied the article and distributed it throughout Ichilov Hospital.

"The strategy paid off. Someone faxed me the report anonymously. Immediately after, I sent a copy to the State Comptroller's Office and requested that it reopen an investigation into the Rabin murder. They replied that there already was an official investigation and it would be pointless to open another one."

Vesti: "Why is Amir keeping quiet? Doesn't he know someone else shot Rabin?"

Gefen: "He must know. Amir was arrested and not permitted visitors for a month. Why, if he was cooperating with investigators? Noam Friedman, who shot seven people in Hebron, cooperated and was allowed to see a lawyer the next day. It took the Shabak a month to persuade Amir to cooperate. And did he ever, after that!

"I sat in most of the sessions of his trial and every time his lawyers made a strong point in his defense, it was he who cut them off, shouting, "I killed him. I did it by myself." It was obvious overplay by Amir. But it doesn't matter what he says. I have documents that disprove him and that are strong enough to warrant opening a new investigation of the assassination. But the government will never let that happen."

THE GUN

Immediately after the shooting, a witness, Noam Kedem, told Reuters, "I heard, like, four, five shots then I saw Rabin collapse." He was one of several witnesses, including policeman Yossi Smadja, who heard five shots. Rabin, according to this account, didn't collapse until after the fourth or fifth shot.

Reinterviewed by *Hatikshoret* Magazine in May 1997, Kedem added another vignette; "I saw a gun clip on the ground. I kicked it towards all the bodyguards." It's possible that amidst all the hubbub, a policeman or bodyguard lost a clip. But there's another possibility. *Maariv* reporter Boaz Gaon, who phoned me after reading the *Hatikshoret* piece, reacted: "It's a strange story. It sounds like there could have been a second gun involved."

This is the thesis of researcher Natan Gefen and a theory presented to the court at Amir's trial by his attorney Gabi Shahar. In short, Amir shot his blank and the real murderer took advantage of the chaos after to shoot Rabin.

The thesis is contradicted by the disturbing account of Yevgeny Furman, an outpatient at Ichilov Hospital who told a Reuters' reporter that he saw Rabin in the emergency room; his eyes were closed and he was bleeding from the back and chest. If there was a frontal chest wound, Amir didn't cause it because he did not shoot from the front. On the other hand, because the chest wound left no bullet hole in Rabin's clothing, it couldn't have occurred in the chaos of the Kings of Israel Square parking lot.

Furman's testimony, combined with that of Drs. Barabash, Gutman, Sneh and the unnamed pathologist revealed in a deposition to the Supreme Court, who told a witness Rabin was shot three times, is powerful proof that a second gun killed Rabin. But if so, how do we explain the fact that the two bullets pulled out of Rabin's body matched Amir's gun in ballistics test?

We look for the answer first in the Israel Police Ballistics Laboratory report prepared by ballistics expert Bernard Shechter. He was given a veritable arsenal of ammunition and weaponry to test beginning with Amir's gun. He complained that he should have been given the gun with a bullet still in the chamber, as is standard procedure. He reported that Amir's gun contained eight bullets. "Four were regular bullets, four were Silver-Tip hollowpoints."

Rabin was supposedly killed by two hollow points and Rubin shot by a regular bullet. According to the conclusions of the Shamgar Commission, first Amir shot a hollowpoint at Rabin, a regular bullet at Rubin and another hollowpoint at Rabin. At Amir's trial Shechter testified that, "The first two bullets loaded were hollowpoints, followed by a regular bullet." Amir objected to Shechter's tests, insisting that he got the order wrong.

Perhaps ballistics testing is not infallible in this area. However, there was no easy escape for the conspirators in another area of testing. Silver-Tip hollowpoints are often manufactured with a small metal pellet in the tip, which significantly increases damage to the body. Amir testified that he used the most powerful bullets he had available, so two should have been found in Rabin's body. Consider Bernard Shechter's testimony at the Amir trial on 3/3/96.

> Defense: "You reported that there were no pellets. Where did you request examination for the pellets?"
>
> Shechter: "In the x-rays. I asked that they be examined to find the pellets in the body. I don't recall precisely when I made the request but I asked five times after I saw the ammunition and saw the pellet in four other bullets. So, I requested that the pathologist, Dr. Hiss, please check the x-ray and perhaps find the pellet. He said he checked and checked and didn't find it."

The next day, Dr. Hiss testified about the missing pellets, "Other than the two bullets I removed from the body of the deceased, there were no other foreign particles." Thus, Amir did not use the most damaging bullets at his disposal.

And now the official line becomes downright implausible. Shortly after Amir was arrested, the police raided his parents' home looking for weapons and ammunition. They left empty-handed. Two days later, the Shabak conducted its own search and came up with enough materiel to supply a small militia. It was found in an attic above Yigal's brother Hagai's room.

Hagai was accused and later convicted of hollowing out the bullets that killed Rabin. He received a light, seven year sentence based on his testimony that he had no idea his brother intended to murder anyone with the bullets... as if there is any other good reason for doctoring the ammunition.

Other researchers have been most intrigued by the fact that Shechter found two blank bullets in Hagai's arsenal and a silencer. I am more perplexed by all the rest. Here is a partial list of bullets from Hagai's armory sent to Shechter to test:

- 5 Silver-Tip (hollowpoint) bullets manufactured by Winchester.

- A package of 380 Winchester Automatic Super-X bullets. (The two bullets found in Rabin's body were Silver-Tip (hollowpoints) manufactured by Winchester.)

Which brings us to the confusion. If Hagai Amir had hundreds of factory-made hollowpoint bullets in his attic, why would he need to hollow out his brother's bullets? The answer is he didn't. The bullets shot at Rabin were already hollowed out by Winchester. The power of these bullets are commonly enhanced by the addition of a small metal pellet inserted into the tip. These were not found in Rabin's body.

To sidestep these problems, the official version has Hagai Amir further hollowing out manufactured hollowpoints and in doing so, removing the small metal pellet. Now why would he do such a thing? Winchester doesn't need his help to beef up its bullets and by removing the metal pellet, he'd achieve the opposite effect.

Dr. Hiss only adds to the confusion when, in the same session, he testifies that the second bullet which hit Rabin was shot horizontally. Amir backed him up later when he testified that he never lowered his gun. But the Shamgar Commission concluded that Amir shot Rabin from above the second time while he was prone on the ground. Until Yoram Rubin renounced all of his previous testimony about how he was shot, the state's case rested, for much of the trial, on the peculiar testimony of police officer Yisrael Gabai who had quite a tale to tell.

Defense: "Do you recall testifying that you saw the defendant holding his gun at a 45 degree angle?"

Gabai: "I recall. I don't recall giving a statement to the police to the same effect. I don't know why I didn't tell this to the police."

Defense: "How come no other policeman said the same thing about the angle?"

Gabai: "Ask them."

Defense: "How can it be that after three months yours is the only testimony in court recalling the defendant holding the gun at a 45 degree angle?"

Gabai: "I told what I saw. As for the other policemen, ask them."

Defense: "You meant, 45 degrees from the ground."

Gabai: "Yes. While he held the gun in that position, no one was on top of him yet. While I was running at him, I saw the defendant standing with the gun pointed at 45 degrees towards the ground. I don't know how many people were beside the prime minister but not one jumped on him, though they were only a meter's distance from him."

Defense: "So you're saying the gun held by the defendant was pointed to the ground?"

Gabai: "True."

So ends part one of Gabai's testimony. In contradiction of a dozen or so witnesses who saw Amir pounced on immediately after the first shot, Gabai insists no one touched him and he stood alone shooting down on the fallen Rabin and Rubin. If believed, Gabai is the only eye-witness to the murder who saw things this way. But there were more problems with his testimony than solutions, the first and most obvious being, why didn't the bodyguards do their duty vis á vis Amir? So, the court eventually rejected Gabai's testimony that an unimpeded Amir shot down and accepted Rubin's newfound version that Amir, in fact, did shoot horizontally. Now to Act Two of Officer Gabai's illuminating testimony.

Defense: "You told the court that you were ordered to look for bullet cartridges."

Gabai: "Correct. I found a 9mm cartridge but the area commander told me to look for .22mm cartridges."

Defense: "You saw the gun before you went looking for the cartridges."

Gabai: "As soon as the defendant was down, the gun was taken by an anti-terror officer. I saw the gun."

He then testified that the gun was taken by a police officer of anti-terror unit. This will be significant shortly.

Defense: "But you didn't get a close look at the gun."

Gabai: "Before I found the cartridge, I could tell what kind of a gun it was."

Defense: "And you couldn't tell what kind of cartridge."

Gabai: "I asked the area commander why on earth he told me to look for a .22mm cartridge."

Defense: "And the cartridge you found was right beside the prime minister's car."

Gabai: "Correct."

Defense: "And it had to be from the gun that shot the prime minister."

Gabai: "I didn't know then. I found a cartridge and I kept it."

Defense: "So why didn't you ask the area commander why you're looking for a .22mm if you already found a different gauge?"

Gabai: "No. No, I didn't see the gun and I didn't know what gauge it was. I heard three shots and I didn't know if the bodyguards or police shot them. I thought the actual gun the prime minister was shot with was a .22mm and I understood this from the area commander."

Quite a quick about-turn. Gabai first saw the gun and then he didn't. He first thought the bullets must be 9mm and then he didn't. Clearly if the area commander ordered him to look for a .22mm bullet at that moment, there must have been a good reason. But the defense pursued it and failed to extract it from Gabai. Exasperated, Amir's attorney tried a new line of questioning but inexplicably failed to properly follow up.

Defense: "Did you ask the area commander if you should also look for a .22mm gun?"

Gabai: "I didn't ask."

Defense: "Were you forewarned that there was suspicion of trouble at the rally."

Gabai: "Yes, but from Arabs, not an attack on the prime minister from one of the crowd."

Defense: "You didn't speak about potential suspects in the crowd."

Gabai: "No."

Quite a police force. Amir was told at the rally by a member of Likud youth that word was out that Itamar Ben Gvir, a well-publicized enemy of Rabin, had vowed to kill him that evening. The Likud youth told Amir that he had already reported the threat to the police. So why wasn't this death threat from a serious and dangerous enemy of Rabin's taken in correct perspective by the police? Why wasn't Gabai, and presumably all other officers, forewarned to look for a potential assassin from the crowd and to apprehend Ben Gvir on the spot?

Amir's attorney attempted to draw the answer out of police officer Yoav Gazit and received a remarkable piece of testimony that was totally ignored after.

Defense: "When you interrogated the defendant on 3/12, the name Itamar Ben Gvir came up."

Gazit: "We know who he is. He has no connection to the incident. Yigal connected him to the incident but later recanted. He gave all kinds of theories to the Shabak... He said that Avishai Raviv passed on blank bullets to Itamar Ben Gvir and that it was done in coordination with the Shabak..."

Defense: "We have a report that the Shabak was responsible for the (police) investigation. Do you know why?"

Gazit: "No idea, but the Shabak was the dominant factor at certain points in the investigation."

Defense: "Why did the Shabak receive responsibility for the investigation?"

Gazit: "I'm not authorized to tell you..."

Defense: "How did you feel about the Shabak's role?"

Gazit: "I didn't appreciate it."

Amir, in fact, almost never theorized in all his testimony. His statement that Avishai Raviv passed blank bullets to Ben Gvir under instructions from the Shabak is an extremely rare glimpse into what secrets Amir may be holding onto. It is the first and only time that he connects Raviv, the Shabak, a potential assassin and blank bullets together. Amir, however momentarily, believed that a second "assassin," already reported to the police was at the rally carrying a gun loaded with blanks supplied by Avishai Raviv. Were these the 22 mm cartridges Gazit was told to look for?

The court did not allow exploration of such "side" issues as the area commander's orders to find 22 mm cartridges because Bernard Shechter testified that the bullets pulled out of Rabin's body by the pathologist Dr. Hiss ballistically matched Amir's gun. The problem with this assumption is that Hiss had no idea what happened to the bullets after he put them in a safe. He admitted to the court. "A policeman took the bullets I removed from Rabin and transferred them to the police laboratory the next day. I don't know his name and I don't recall what he looked like, but they were transferred."

The aptly named Dr. Hiss testified that the bullets were given to a policeman. But Yoram Rubin, Rabin's bodyguard, testified that, "The bullets and clothes were taken by Yuval Schwartz, a friend of mine from work." Straight to the point, Rubin said the bullets were taken by a Shabak agent. So which was it, a policeman according to Dr. Hiss or a Shabak agent, according to Rubin?

In fact, there are no records to properly explain how the bullets got from the safe to the police laboratory. The chain of evidence was broken and there was no proof that the bullets tested were the same bullets Hiss said he removed from Rabin's body. And there is yet another unsolvable difficulty. Dr. Kluger also testified that he removed the bullets from Rabin. Both doctors can't be right.

If the reader thinks the testimony regarding who took the bullets to the police laboratory is contradictory, consider the fate of the gun itself. We begin with the lengthy testimony of Police Supervisor Yamin Yitzhak, head of the anti-terrorism unit at the rally.

> Yitzhak: "I was coming down the stairs behind the stage. I was two or three steps from the bottom when I heard three shots in a row. I ran quickly down... I saw a guy in a blue shirt holding a black gun and I jumped on him. Seconds passed between the shots and when I apprehended the guy. I hit him in his hand, pulled his hair and wrestled him to the ground. Then others joined in. The gun was still in his hand."

> Court: "From the moment of physical contact, there were no other shots?"

> Yitzhak: "After then, no. The gun was cocked, the clip was inside. I grabbed the defendant's right hand, knowing the hammer of the gun was cocked. I twisted his hand and took the gun from him quickly. Someone from the service (Shabak) arrived and asked me for the gun, I refused to hand it over, and a give-me-the-gun war erupted. I was holding on to the gun while my thumb was blocking the hammer. The Shabak agent insisted I give him the gun and I said no, because it wasn't disarmed. I was surrounded by people and I shouted at them to cuff him (Amir)... After he was taken away, the Shabak guy persisted in harassing me. I went looking for the area commander and asked him to get this guy off my back. He was a Shabak agent but I don't know his name. All the while, he was trying to get the gun. After the defendant was pinned to the wall, I showed the gun to the area commander. I took it aside to check it. I removed the bullet from the chamber and it fell to the ground where I couldn't see it. I asked for a nylon bag, put the gun and clip in it and shoved it into the front of my pants. After a search of the area was organized, I gave the gun to the investigations officer, Deputy Inspector Naftali."

> Defense: "How far away from the defendant were you when you heard the shots?"

Yitzhak: "About from here to the defense table (3 meters)."

Defense: "And the defendant was still standing when you got to him."

Yitzhak: "He was still standing. There was someone beside him wearing a grey shirt or jacket."

At this point, Yigal Amir had had enough. He cross-examined Yitzhak with vigor. He held out his right hand as if a gun was in it and asked Yitzhak to demonstrate how he took the gun from him. The demonstration was different than his testimony. Instead of pulling his hair, he knocked Amir in the nape with his right hand and grabbed the gun with his left. He justified the awkward position by explaining that he was ambidextrous. Amir burst out in anger;

Amir: "You say you took the gun from me. I say it fell on the ground and I heard it as it landed."

Yitzhak: "I'm positive I took it."

Amir (to the court): "There were two guards accompanying the prime minister. And you say they did not try to apprehend me until you ran all the way from the steps. That sounds weird."

Yitzhak: "I think the distance between the place the bodyguards were and where I was, I was on the way down the steps and the distance was reduced, I just remember there were other people there, I took the gun from you, for sure. I punched you, for sure. I know what I did. Maybe there were other people with me. They came, it was a matter of seconds, no, less. If someone else was there, he neglected to take the weapon. I did that. I didn't see the prime minister but I was really close to him. Really close."

Third year law student Amir had succeeded in totally rattling Yitzhak. Now he closed in for the kill.

Amir: "Maybe you picked it up off the ground and thought you took it from me?"

Yitzhak: "No."

Amir: "People jumped on me, then there were two shots. Lots of people jumped at the same time. I dropped the gun so they wouldn't shoot me. I heard the sound of it hitting the ground."

Yitzhak: "No. I can tell you definitely that first I heard three shots and in a matter of seconds, after the three shots, I got to you, dropped you on the ground and took your gun."

Defense: "You say you did what you did but maybe he really did release the gun first."

Yitzhak: "I'll say it again, from the moment I saw the guy, it was seconds until I took the gun from him."

Now what is going on here? Supervisor Yitzhak is a high ranking officer and he insists he took Amir's gun from his hand. And he recalls the moment in great detail including in his testimony the fact that he placed his thumb between the hammer and cartridge, disarmed the gun and gave it to Officer Naftali. And while all this was going on, one Shabak agent was desperately trying to get him to hand the gun over to him.

Could he have been be lying? He had better have been for the state's sake because he was insisting that he ran from three meter's distance, a matter of seconds, and Amir was still on his feet. In direct contradiction to all previous testimony, including Amir's, he said Amir shot three times without any interference from Rabin's bodyguards whatsoever. And he insisted that the gun he wrestled from Amir was the gun that did the shooting. So why would the Shabak be so desperate to keep it out of the hands of the police?

The answer, if Yitzhak was telling the truth, is that the honest police examiners were going to discover, as they did, that Amir shot only once and that the bullets in Rabin's body didn't match this gun. Now we will try and work out if Yitzhak was telling the truth according to other witnesses.

- Shabak officer Adi Azulai related in his police statement of the night of the murder that he saw the gun fall, that HE found the gun on the ground, that there was a bullet in the chamber and that a police officer took it from him.

- Police unit officer Avi Cohen reported, the same night, that he saw the gun fall as Amir was pounced on.

- An unnamed Police officer from the Yarkon district headquarters reported, the same night, that he also saw the gun fall.

- Officer Yisrael Gabai of the Yarkon district headquarters, testified at Amir's trial that he saw Yamin Yitzhak take the gun from Amir's hand.

- Deputy Inspector Naftali testified that other policemen told him they took the gun from Amir. In the same session, he added the enticing fact that a watch and pair of glasses were found on the ground at the murder scene and their owners have never been found.

- Police Officer Yisrael Gabai testified that he saw the gun taken from Amir's hand.

- Shabak agent "Shin" (Sh) testified that agent "Bet" (B) Benny Lahav, a high ranking Shabak official, demanded the gun from Yamin Yitzhak.

- Shabak agent "Aleph" (A) testified that he saw the argument between "Bet," Lahav and the policeman holding the gun. Lahav wanted the gun but the policeman wouldn't give it to him. Lahav examined the gun, checked the bullets and returned it to the policeman.

- Police officer Avi Yahav testified that he saw a policeman holding the gun, saying it was Amir's.

- Police officer Efron Moshe testified that the gun was on the ground and the police picked it up.

- Police officer Avraham Cohen initially testified that the gun was forced out of Amir's hand, then he retracted his words, testifying that Amir dropped the gun. He concluded that Deputy Inspector Naftali eventually got possession of it.

There you have it. Two Shabak officers backed Yamin Yitzhak's testimony about fighting over the gun with a high ranking Shabak official. Four policemen testified that either Yitzhak or another police officer wrestled the gun out of Amir's hand. On the other hand, one Shabak agent claimed he found the gun on the ground and three policemen testified that the gun fell to the ground.

So who is one going to believe? All of them if there was a second gun. The few researchers who have examined the evidence closely are divided over when the fatal bullets were shot. Those who believe Rabin was murdered in his car or at the hospital point to the car door closing before anyone was supposed to be inside, the unexplainably long ride to the hospital, the police lab tests proving there were two point blank or near point blank shots at the back, the account of Yevgeny Furman to Reuters that he saw Rabin in the emergency room of Ichilov with a chest wound, and the doctors who reported a third chest wound.

Those who insist he was shot at the parking lot of the rally stress the three shots heard by many people, and the ample, contradictory testimony of police and Shabak officers just reviewed which indicates to them the likelihood of a second gun at the scene of the murder. The truth may yet turn out to be a combination of both scenarios.

THE THIRD
SHOT AT RABIN

The conspiracy theory of the shooting of Yitzhak Rabin is now substantiated. According to the Shamgar Commission Report, the testimony at the trial of Yigal Amir, and the Kempler film, the alleged assassin Yigal Amir shot Rabin twice in the back. But what if Rabin had a third wound in the chest? That Amir could not have done from behind... This is precisely the case.

The story of the discovery of the third chest wound begins when determined amateur researcher, Natan Gefen, showed me a copy of the last page of a report signed by Dr. Mordecai Gutman at 22:30 on Ichilov Hospital stationery. Of Rabin's wounds Dr. Gutman wrote,"Bullet wound in upper lung lobe exit wound of 2.5-3 cm in the direction of D5-6 with a shattering of the vertebrae."

The document was remarkable to say the least. For one thing, no other source ever mentioned that Rabin's spinal cord was shattered. I called a Doctor for a better understanding of what Dr. Gutman wrote. He said, "What is being described is a shot to the chest which entered and exited the lung, shattering vertebrae numbers D5-6 in the upper back."

Could such a wound have been caused by a shot to the back? "Not likely. To do so, the bullet would have had to have entered the back, pierced the upper lobe of the lung, then returned to exit the lung before smashing into the backbone. Bullets have been known to take unexpected paths but on first consideration, this doesn't seem feasible."

I was totally stumped by the report because it contradicted the honest testimony of Chief Lieutentant Baruch Gladstein of the Israel Police Forensic and Materials Laboratory at the trial of Yigal Amir. After examining Rabin's suit and shirt, he determined that the prime minister was shot twice in the back from point blank and near point blank range. He would not have missed a bullet hole in the chest nor, after what he revealed would he likely have lied in court about it. I found the solution on May 16—but before revealing it, we'll jump ahead to May 17.

I referred Gefen to two journalists, Boaz Gaon of *Maariv* and Jay Bushinsky of NBC. Both took the document to Ichilov where hospital officials confirmed its veracity. However, they added, according to Bushinsky, a cautionary explanation that, "This is the last page of a six page medical procedural report which was intended only for the perusal of Rabin's immediate family. Without understanding the first five pages, the last page is out of context and meaningless."

Gutman's handwritten report was never released to anyone except Leah Rabin. Instead, a typed report signed by Drs. Gutman, Hausner and Kluger was released publicly one day after the assassination. But Natan Gefen had all six pages of the original report in his possession.

On May 17, the doctor and his wife, a police medic with much experience dealing directly with bullet wounds, joined me for a professional reading of Dr. Gutman's report, the public procedural report, the pathologist's summation and the court testimony of the surgeon, Dr. Kluger, and the pathologist, Dr. Hiss.

The very first line of Dr. Gutman's report states that Rabin was brought into the emergency room with "no pulse or heartbeat and suffering from priapism." The doctor immediately explained, "Priapism means he had a severe injury to his nervous system."

The next day he faxed me a page from a medical report which read, "In the male, check for priapism (sustained erection of the penis), which, when present, is a characteristic sign of spinal cord injury."

His wife, the medic, noted, "To me, this is proof that the report is genuine. Considering the sensitivity of the nation at that moment, no doctor would have reported priapism unless he was being honest in his observations."

The report then describes procedures which succeeded in reviving Rabin. His pulse and heartbeat returned and he was rushed to the operating room. There, padding was removed and damage caused by a bullet hole from the right upper lung which shattered vertebrae D5-6 described, as well as a wound from the flank which passed through the spleen and lodged in the lower left lung. The latter wound caused little bleeding and was not fatal. A total of eight units of blood were transfused during the operation on the wounds. The former wound to the chest and spinal cord ultimately was the cause of death. Despite Ichilov's later protest, there was nothing out of context in the final page of Dr. Gutman's report. He describes a chest wound whose path led to a shattered spinal cord.

The surgeon, Dr. Gutman, signed his report at 22:30 of November 4. The pathologist, Dr. Hiss, began work on Rabin's body approximately ninety minutes later. Then a most remarkable change took place; the priaspism, chest wound and shattered spinal cord disappeared. He concluded that, "There was no damage to the spinal cord." Both he and Dr. Kluger so testified at the trial of Yigal Amir in March, 1995.

As did the joint public report of Drs. Gutman, Hausner and Kluger one day later. Gone were the priapism and chest wound and the shattered vertebrae were altered not too discreetly. Vertebrae 5-6 became rib numbers 5 and 6. The new version of events had Rabin shot in the back, the bullet passing between ribs 5-6 and lodging in the upper lobe of the right lung.

So what happened between 11:30 PM and 1:00 AM? The answer is the murder itself.

The Beginning of the Mystery

What to do about the contradiction between Chief Lieutenant Gladstein's report of two bullets through the back of Rabin's clothing and Dr. Gutman's description of a fatal chest wound?

On May 2, I received a visit from the researcher of this book, an energetic teenager, Yechiel Mann, who had previously e-mailed me that he had been gathering evidence since the very night of the assassination. He left me a videotape of Channel One's coverage of the assassination that he had had the foresight to record on the night of the murder. It was almost four hours long and I put it aside for the near future.

The next Friday evening, I received a visit from Zeev Barcella, the editor of the 200,000 circulation Russian-language paper *Vreyma* and a staff reporter Emma Sodnikov. Joining us, quite accidentally was a family friend, a Russian-born pharmacist, Assia Miller. During the interview, I gave Zeev, Natan Gefen's phone number and described the document he had uncovered. Zeev related a relevant story:

> "The morning after the assassination, a Russian-speaking operating room nurse called me and said, 'There's something wrong. The media isn't reporting Rabin's real wounds. His spine was shattered and they're saying it wasn't.' Ninety minutes later she called me back sounding terrified and told me, 'I didn't call you before. You never heard from me,' and then she put down the phone."

I decided to present Zeev with the most perplexing piece of evidence I had acquired. In one of the most bizarre episodes of the assassination night, while Rabin was being operated on, his aide Eitan Haber rifled through his pockets, pulling out whatever was inside. Among the items he recovered was a bloody song sheet Rabin had placed in his chest pocket. Within the bloodstain was a black, nearly perfectly round hole.

I had gone on television the previous October and claimed there was a bullet hole in the sheet of paper. Unfortunately for me, the sheet was folded in four and the hole was in only one section. The television reporter jumped on the error, claimed the hole was a bloodstain and I lost a lot of credibility.

But, as Assia noted, that hole was no bloodstain. Blood isn't black nor does it clot in near pefect circles the size of a bullet. Zeev guessed, "It looks like someone tried to burn a hole into the sheet, then thought better of it and stopped." Emma concurred, "That would explain the black color."

Bullet hole or not, the bloody song sheet more than merely indicated that Rabin was bleeding from the chest. Two weeks later Dr. Barshov explained, "It's just not probable that a back wound would be absorbed from paper in the chest pocket." So how did the blood get on the sheet?

On May 15, I received a remarkable document. It was an appeal submitted to the Supreme Court of Israel on 6/31/96. Within, a taxi driver felt, as a good citizen, that he had to relay important testimony concerning the Rabin assassination. I add, the taxi driver sought no publicity, his name remains unknown to the public and people do not present evidence to the Supreme Court on a lark. I further add, the conclusions of the Supreme Court's session regarding the following testimony has never been released to the public.

Included in the request to submit new evidence are the following passages:

"According to the declaration of the witness, the prime minister was shot by a third bullet of a different caliber from the other two bullets."

"I, T— [full name hidden because the witness fears retaliation] declare the following to be truthful."

On 3/27/96 the verdict in the trial of Yigal Amir was read.

"I am a taxi driver and at the time the verdict was announced over the radio, I was driving a tanned passenger, about 50 years old with silver-rimmed glasses from Yaffa to Ichilov Hospital in Tel Aviv.

"After hearing the Amir verdict, the passenger began a conversation with me. He said Yigal Amir was right and according to the facts he couldn't have killed the prime minister even if he wanted to. I asked the passenger what he meant and he said one bullet was shot from less than 20 cm away, the other, even closer and a third bullet of a different caliber was shot point blank.

"I told him those facts weren't published anywhere and that I didn't believe him. At this point the passenger showed me his identity card which read that he was a pathologist. I have forgotten his name but it might be Peretz. (In Hebrew Peretz and Hiss contain three similar looking letters. (B.C.)

"I was surprised to see he was a pathologist and then he told me he examined Rabin's body on the night of the murder.

"I said that on the night of the murder, another pathologist announced on television that Rabin was shot by two bullets. I asked him if it's possible that after the annoucement someone could have got to the operating room and shot Rabin again. The passenger didn't answer me but he smiled. I asked him if he was certain there were three bullets and he replied he examined Rabin's body and found three entrance wounds.

"In the course of the journey, the passenger told me that there was another dead body in the hospital that night and that according to his clothing and other signs he was positive it was of a bodyguard from the event that night. He told me that the government wasn't telling the whole story. He added that there was something about the prime minister's clothes they weren't telling either but he didn't elaborate.

"That is my testimony and it is the truth."

On May 16, I was reading the protocols of Yigal Amir's trial and was startled by the testimony of Rabin's bodyguard, Yoram Rubin. While Rabin was in the operating room, his driver, Menachem Damti, rushed up to the "wounded" bodyguard Yoram Rubin and took his gun from him. Rubin testified that, "I gave it to him because I wasn't myself and I was worried that an Arab or someone from the minorities would take it." One would not expect many Arabs to be admitted to the area where the Prime Minister and his bodyguard were situated. I couldn't understand why Rubin handed his gun to Damti, nor what he needed it for at that moment. Rubin's gun is never mentioned again in the protocols.

On May 16, I finally watched Yechial's videotape of Channel One's coverage of the assassination night. At about 11:30, the director of Ichilov Hospital, Dr. Gabi Barabash, announced the cause of Rabin's death:

"The Prime Minister arrived at the hospital without pulse or heartbeat. He was clinically dead. We succeeded in reviving him and transfused 21 units of blood but the wounds were too severe and he succumbed to them."

"What were the wounds?" asked the television reporter Chaim Yavin.

"There was a wound to the spleen and a gaping hole in the chest leading to the backbone. The first bullet was not necessarily fatal. The other bullet tore apart vessels leading to the heart and shattered his spinal cord...The Prime Minister died of spinal shock."

At 12:45, Health Minister Ephraim Sneh appeared on television and pronounced the cause of Rabin's death. He prefaced the announcement with the words, "As a result of incitement, Prime Minister Rabin died tonight... He took three bullets, one in the chest, one in the stomach and one in the spine."

At 11:30, the director general of Ichilov Hospital announced that Rabin was shot twice. Barely an hour later, the Minister of Health, surely in an informed, official capacity announced a third bullet. But both are in agreement on two essential facts: Rabin was shot in the chest and his spinal cord was shattered.

These facts were never again mentioned. By the next day and henceforth, the official story was that Yigal Amir shot Rabin in the back twice injuring his flank, waist, diaphram and lungs. But never, not in the Shamgar Report nor at Amir's trial is there a word about a chest wound or shattered spine... because if those were the wounds, Amir would have had to have shot from the front and Rabin would have collapsed on the spot from the severed nerves. The Kempler film shows Amir shooting from behind and Rabin continuing to walk after the shot.

I sat there thinking. Over and over I considered that Yigal Amir shot from behind. He could not have caused the chest wound. But what of Chief Lieutenant Gladstein's testimony that Rabin's clothing bore the holes of only two shots, neither from the front?

Direct evidence of a third shot now came from the health minister, the director general of Ichilov Hospital, testimony to the Supreme Court, from Dr. Gutman's signed report, and from the nurse who called Zeev Barcella. That was overwhelming. There had to have been a third shot from the front. But how?

Then it hit me. I called cameraman Alon Eilat and said, "Eureka. (Cliche or not, I really quoted Archimedes). I know how it happened."

He rushed over and looked at the filmed testimony of Sneh and Barabash for the first time. He said in reaction, "You can't get higher level testimony than that. There had to have been a frontal chest wound."

"So," I asked, "What about Gladstein's evidence based on two bullets in the back of Rabin's suit?"

Alon thought hard and finally gave up.

I said, "The only possibility is that Rabin wasn't wearing his clothes when he was shot in the chest. It had to have been done in the hospital."

We went over the evidence and came up with the most likely scenario. Rabin arrived alive at the hospital. He took two point blank shots in the back during the car ride to Ichilov and somehow survived them. When the doctors revived him, the conspirators panicked and used one of their guns to finish him off with a bullet through the chest which shattered his spine.

It was at this point that the coverup began. The conspirators realized the fatal flaw in the final shot. Rabin wasn't wearing his clothes and there was no hole in the front of his suit or shirt. So they rifled through his pockets, found the song sheet and tried to burn a bullet hole through it, probably with a cigarette. Quickly, they realized how futile that was and abandoned the idea. There was no believable way to add a third shot to the clothes or their contents.

Instead, they threatened the doctors and staff to lie. One can only imagine the brutal threats. We had a hint of them in May 1996 when the news magazine *Zman Tel Aviv* reported that everyone on duty at Ichilov saving Rabin, seventeen people, received anonymous death threats by mail. The first to be threatened that night was the pathologist and probable taxi passenger Dr. Hiss. By 1 AM, he got rid of the truthful conclusions of Drs. Gutman, Sneh and Barabash and invented a whole new story deleting the chest and spinal wounds. And from that point on, the coverup continued. Murder threats from people who have nothing to lose can keep a lot of people quiet, even and especially cabinet ministers.

MISCELLANEOUS MYSTERIES

After over 18 months of research, the proof of a conspiracy to murder Yitzhak Rabin seemed nearly complete. A few loose ends would have to be tied and then the case would close like a finely wrapped gift. I sent my researcher, Yechiel Mann to the national newspaper archive, Beit Ariellah to find citations for two bothersome mysteries. The first assignment was to find an article that I was repeatedly told appeared in *Maariv* two months after the murder. In it, the reporter provides proof in the form of three letters between the police and Shabak that Yigal Amir was arrested on June 27, 1995 on suspicion of planning Rabin's murder and released on July 1 on the orders of the Shabak.

The second assignment was especially important; I had previously written that the Chief Surgeon of Ichilov, Dr. Yehuda Skornik, had said that, based on gunpowder traces found in Rabin's wounds, and the shape of the wounds themselves, Rabin was shot point blank. I had forgotten where I read the information, but it had appeared around May 3, 1995 just prior to Amir's appeal.

The trip to the archives was a flop. Yechiel found likely references and when he opened the newspapers to find the stories, they had been cut out. He had found an article on the doctors of Ichilov ripped in two, one half was readable, while the half with information on Dr. Skornik was missing.

The next week, he tried again. This time he was unexplainably met by a woman in her twenties who had a file on the assassination ready for him to look at. She explained that she was doing research on the subject but could not explain how she knew he was also there to do just that. The mystery lady provided some useful peripheral information, but the hard data on Skornik could not be found because his file had seemingly been erased from the computer. The Chief Surgeon of Ichilov no longer existed in Bet Ariella's hard drive. Not a quote, even regarding injuries from traffic accidents, was listed.

So my researcher went investigating, freestyle. He left the archives with photocopies of articles supplied by the helpful woman and a few juicy finds of his own. These articles were unwelcome. Just when I thought I was finally approaching something resembling an airtight scenario, new mysteries emerged, which would require plausible explanations... perhaps in the followup book. I had to admit, the assassination was too complicated to be solved completely, and new information just wouldn't stop coming in. Included in the latest newspaper discoveries are the following questions:

What Does Dr. Yehuda Skornik Know and Why Isn't He Telling?

As Chief Surgeon of Ichilov Hospital, Dr. Skornik was not only privy to Rabin's medical records but was obliged to read every word written by his surgeons about their treatment of him on his final night alive. Yet he did not testify at the Shamgar Commission nor at Amir's trial. Somewhere, I am convinced, a statement by him regarding Rabin's wounds once appeared in the press.

Yechiel called Ichilov Hospital several times to speak to Dr. Skornik. His calls were totally screened by his secretary who would not allow any call through because, "Dr. Skornik is a very busy man."

Why All the Secrecy?

Readers, get ready. On the night of the assassination, Dr Skornik's son Ohad was arrested and charged with being an accessory to Rabin's murder. The scenario is a bit too bizarre; while the Chief Surgeon's staff was working to save Rabin, his son was being sought in connection to his murder. The police suspected that Ohad, a friend of Yigal Amir's from Bar Ilan University, withheld prior knowledge of the assassination. Five days later, he was released from jail.

I asked myself, what are the odds of THIS?

Why Couldn't the Doctors Get their Stories Straight?

Until my researcher brought in his batch of printed trouble for me, I had believed, based on its findings, that the Shamgar Commission knew nothing of Rabin's spinal cord being shattered. But buried in an article about the driver Damti's testimony to the commission is Prof. Gabi Barabash's testimony. It reads:

> "The first bullet caused injury to Rabin's vertebrae and the spinal cord."

The Shamgar Commission was informed, so why didn't they ask the next, most obvious questions: *Was the spinal cord badly damaged and if so, why is Rabin seen on the Kempler film walking after the shot?*

As if I didn't need more proof that Rabin's spine and chest were shot, Yechiel also found the following article from *Maariv* on the day after the murder. Reporters Yossi Levy, Yaacov Galanti and Shira Imerglick wrote, "According to expert sources, the first bullet struck Rabin in the chest and the second in the spinal cord... Amir shot from a distance of two or three meters."

While the experts revealed the crucial wounds to the chest and spine, their order of injury was muddled. But what to make of the two to three meter range? That, as we shall soon see, appears to be raw disinformation.

If Dr. Barabash testified to a spinal wound at Amir's trial, then his testimony never appeared in the protocols. Two other prominent doctors also did not testify at the trial; Dr. Mordechai Gutman, whose original report has Rabin shot in the chest from the front, and the above-named Dr. Yehuda Skornik.

But there was still another doctor who disappeared from the legal arena. Until the stack of clippings arrived from Bet Ariella, I had never heard of him. On 11/6/95, *Maariv* reporter Yisraela Shaked interviewed, Dr. Nir Cohen:

> "a surgical expert who was on duty at the trauma center of the hospital at 21:52 and was the first to tend to Rabin. 'Only after two minutes of resuscitation did I realize the man I was treating was the Prime Minister,' he says.
>
> "I recall hearing a different sounding siren. Immediately after, I saw him transferred from the ambulance to the trauma room. He was pale, had no pulse and was deeply gasping. After beginning resuscitation, I put all the pieces together when I saw his fancy suit and the bodyguard yelling as he came in, 'This is a disaster. This is a disaster.'
>
> "Then the reports arrived by phone and pager that Rabin was on the way to us. They arrived as Rabin was being resuscitated."

We can forgive Dr. Cohen for his one minute error on the time of arrival. BUT, Rabin did not arrive in an ambulance. And it's most unlikely he would mistake a black limousine for an ambulance. Dr. Cohen is not telling the truth.

Rabin was not shot in the face and it's unbelievable that Dr. Cohen would not recognize him immediately. That he eventually figured out who he was by his fancy suit and his screaming bodyguard is implausible.

What is not implausible is that the hospital was only told of Rabin's imminent arrival well after Dr. Cohen had begun treating him. Within this piece of truth may be the reason Dr. Cohen lied, unconvincingly, to *Maariv*.

How Did Damti Get Away With So Many Lies?

Menachem Damti was not supposed to be Rabin's chauffeur on the night of his death. He was a last second replacement for Rabin's regular driver Yeheskiel Sharabi. The real reason for the decision to replace Sharabi with Damti is not hard to imagine, Damti was Peres' regular driver. What is difficult to fathom is how much Damti was allowed to perjure himself.

Let us compare Damti's reality with the facts. Shortly after the murder, Damti told television reporter Rafi Reshef,

> "When the Prime Minister was descending the last step I saw someone on the right lift his hand and start shooting."

Fact: Rabin was not on the steps, he was almost beside the car, three meters away, when he was shot. Amir would not have had the room to shoot him had Rabin still been descending the steps. Nonetheless, as we shall soon see, *Maariv* also adopted this scenario early in the coverup.

> Damti: "The shooter shouted, 'It's nothing, they're not real bullets, they're blanks, this wasn't real.'"

Fact: Quite a mouthful to shout while in the midst of shooting someone. Amir denies shouting anything and almost all witnesses heard similar shouts from the bodyguards.

> Damti: "The truth is that I, myself believed that it was like that, that it wasn't real. Nonetheless, I did what they taught me. I jumped to the steering wheel."

Fact: The Kempler film shows indisputably that Damti did not immediately jump inside the car, rather he stayed outside and played some role in putting Rabin in the vehicle.

> Damti: "After twenty or thirty meters of driving, I asked the Prime Minister, 'Are you hurt?' He answered, 'Yes.' Then I knew it was real and went into action. I asked him, 'Where does it hurt?' He answered, 'Ay, Ay, it hurts in the back but not terribly.' Then I speeded up."

Fact: What we are asked to believe is that Damti was taking a leisurely cruise until he had a conversation with Rabin which finally convinced him to speed the trip up. One of the many suspensions of disbelief required to buy this story is the fact that Yoram Rubin told almost the exact story to the *New York Times* on November 8, 1995, only this time Rabin told HIM he wasn't hurt badly. Unless they took turns asking Rabin the same questions, one or both are engaged in rather blatant falsehoods.

> Damti: "Suddenly there was a barricade in the street. There were policeman manning it. The bodyguard (Rubin) shouted, 'Go, go,' but I stopped briefly and asked one of the policemen to guide me to the hospital."

We now examine what Damti told the Shamgar Commission:

> Damti: "The Prime Minister descended the steps and arrived to within half a meter of his armoured limousine. I opened the door for Mrs. Rabin, then I heard a blast."

Fact: Damti has changed his story. No longer is Rabin on the last step, he is beside the car. But he just can't handle the complications of learning the new version. This time he opens the door for Leah Rabin, who really is on the steps, nine meters away.

> Damti: "I drove away in a hurry. I was going to take Shaul Hamelekh Street, but there were too many people. I wanted to take a shortcut through Bloch Street but there was a police barrier there and I thought the whole street was barricaded. I told the bodyguard all the streets were blocked and he suggested I pick up a policeman to guide us. For some reason I received no communications on the route, as is usually the case. I pushed down on the gas, and despite the delay, arrived at the hospital in a minute and a half."

Fact: Where to begin? Gone is Damti's moving conversation with Rabin. Instead Damti rushes to Bloch Street and sees a police barrier. This is actually what he should have been looking for since the barriers were there to close the street to unauthorized traffic and speed the officials through. Instead, he became worried that the whole street was barricaded. In his previous story to Rafi Reshef, he was more than happy to see the police barricade, and despite protests from Rubin, he stopped and took in a policeman to direct him to the hospital. In this version to the Shamgar Commission, the opposite happened; he didn't want to stop at the barrier, but Rubin suggested bringing in a policeman. We hope he timed himself from the moment he stopped at the police barricade because, he seems to be saying that despite the delay, he arrived at the hospital in a minute and a half, over six minutes before the earliest report of his arrival by anyone else.

Why did the Shamgar Commission let him get away with all this perfidy, contradiction, impossibility and outright balderdash? And why wasn't Damti forced to finally explain why a 700 meter trip to the hospital really took over eight minutes to complete?

And what do we make of this report from *Yediot Ahronot*? It seems Menachem Damti's brother Naftali was also in the sterile zone "on a VIP pass" and "he was the first civilian to overcome Amir." Do the Damti brothers deserve the same infamy as the Amir brothers?

Was it Disinformation or Was There a Shot from the Front?

I couldn't believe the sketch. The morning of the murder, *Maariv* reconstructed the event in a sketch made by Eldad Zakobitz. The assassin was standing on the sidewalk across the driveway where Rabin's car was parked and was shooting at Rabin's chest from the front, from a distance of about three metres. The sketch accompanied the eye-witness report of journalist Yoav Limor,

> "Then it happened. The terrible moment which I will never forget in my life. Suddenly I heard a shot, then another, then another. I stood a meter, perhaps two behind the Prime Minister with Aliza Goren... They took the gun away from the youth who stood on the opposite sidewalk at a distance of five or six meters from the Prime Minister... A minute after, a police officer said it was a blank gun and nothing happened to Rabin."

The next day, *Maariv* featured a full page sketch by Zakobitz. This time the assassin stood against the wall opposite the stairs and shot Rabin from a good three meters away, but behind him.

My first instinct was that this must be disinformation. My phone conversation with Zakobitz seemed to confirm the thought.

> BC: "Why did you originally draw the sketch of the assassin shooting from the front?"

> Zakobitz: "I was working with the information we had and it turned out to be wrong. The next day I drew it right."

> BC: "Actually, your sketch is a very accurate depiction of what Yoav Limor wrote. I can understand the error if he was mistaken. But the next day's sketch was not right. You have the shooter firing from three meters away beside the steps."

> Zakobitz: "That's what everyone thought had happened. The facts weren't clear yet."

BC: "Dozens of people had reported that Amir shot Rabin from a meter away by the next day. Yours is the only recreation having him shoot from three meter's distance."

Zakobitz: "I hope you're not writing that this was a Shabak murder."

BC: "That's the way the evidence is pointing."

Zakobitz: "Nonsense. There is a right and left wing in this country and the left doesn't kill. Only the right does. Rabin was killed by a religious zealot."

BC: "I have hospital reports..."

Zakobitz: "Hospitals all lie. I was in one and they scribbled garbage."

BC: "And I have police reports..."

Zakobitz: "They lie too. Rabin was murdered by the right and no one else."

My conversation with Yoav Limor was more dignified.

BC: "You wrote that you were standing a meter or two behind Rabin when he was shot."

Limor: "Yes, there's a photo which proves it."

BC: "Then you must have been right beside Yigal Amir?"

Limor: "I was told he was just in front of me."

BC: "So how could you think the shots came from six meters away in front of Rabin?"

Limor: "First of all, the distance wasn't six meters. I went back there and measured and there is only three meters from where the shots actually came from and where I thought they came from."

BC: "Still, three meters is a big difference from where you were standing, maybe less than a meter from Amir. Could you really have made that kind of mistake?"

Limor: "I must have, obviously. I really am not familiar with weapons and there was a lot of hysteria at the time."

BC: "You don't have to be an expert to hear a noise. I'd hate to drive with you if that's how you judge distances. Look, what if I told you, you might have been right. I have solid medical proof that Rabin suffered a frontal chest wound. Maybe, you did hear the fatal shot correctly."

Limor: "What kind of proof?"

BC: The first Ichilov surgeon's report recorded statements by Ephraim Sneh and Gabi Barabash. They also report a frontal wound.

Is There More To The Feeling Than Meets The Eye?

One of the questions I am often asked is if I think the organizers of the rally, Chich Lahat and Jean Frydman were involved in the conspiracy. I reply that don't know but they sure had strange roles in the peace process.

Lahat was the Likud mayor of Tel Aviv, yet once Rabin announced his "peace" with the PLO, Lahat more than merely jumped on the opposition bandwagon. He organized a group of washed-up former IDF generals as a pro-peace lobbying group and was apparently rewarded with an executive position on Jean Freidman's Ifshar Fund.

Frydman is a French television mogul closely connected to Shimon Peres. He spent $6 million of his own money to fund a massive public relations campaign on behalf of the peace agreements. Tens of thousands of road signs and wall posters flooded the country reading, 'We Want Peace.' Each and every one of them was victimized by grafitti artists who added one word to the message, 'We Want Another Peace.'

Frydman founded the Ifshar Fund, supposedly to finance economic projects but it was, in reality, just another push "peace" idea. Lahav was his partner in the scheme. Frydman financed the rally where Rabin was murdered, Lahav arranged the permits and municipal details.

Yediot Ahronot reported, "Jean Frydman will not be interviewed for his reaction to Rabin's death. 'I have such feelings of guilt, I can't sleep,'" he explained.

The same newspaper cornered a quote from Lahat while he was visiting the Rabin family. He said, "I came to shake hands with the family. I didn't say a word, didn't cry. For days I've been crying. I have irrational guilt feelings."

We hope for organizing the fatal rally and nothing more.

More Miscellaneous Amir Questions

What were Amir's intelligence ties? We discover in the clippings that the internal Shabak investigation of the assassination revealed that one of Avishai Raviv's tasks was to recruit Yigal Amir into the service. We also are informed that Amir was tested and found unsuitable.

We also learn from Gabi Bron, *Yediot Ahronot*'s Knesset reporter that, "As an employee of the Liaison Office, he was trained at a security course in shooting and weaponry. In one class he was trained in personal security. The teachers informed the class that the weakest points in an assassination are when the victim enters or leaves a car." A lesson he never forgot?

Who Was That Bearded Man?

Police Officers Moti Sergei and Boaz Haran testified at the Shamgar Commission that they saw Amir talking with a bearded man in a black tee shirt minutes before the shooting. The officers added that it appeared they were acquainted with each other.

At Amir's hearing, *Yediot Ahronot* correspondent Booky Naeh reported, "The murderer of the Prime Minister, Yigal Amir, held an impromptu press conference in the hall of the court house... Amir would not answer the question of who the bearded man was who spoke to him minutes before the murder. The existence of the man was established at the commission of inquiry.

However, at Amir's hearing Reuters reported, "As Amir entered, a bearded man gave him a military salute." The same Reuters, which seemed to have an edge on the reporting, wrote that "Amir was seen talking on a public phone ten minutes before the murder."

Why So Photogenic?

When the 1995-96 Bar Ilan University yearbook was published in May 1996, recipients were shocked to find 24 separate photos of Yigal Amir within. They saw Amir at the study hall, in prayer, in debate. On a campus of 18,000 students, he was singled out as by far the most photogenic.

The university spokesman explained that the yearbook was printed in the US and that they did not have a final say in the editing. So who did?

How Did The Information Leak So Quickly?

On the assassination night, Israel television reported that Amir tried to kill Rabin on two other occasions. My researcher and several correspondents consider this fact most suspicious, first because it was the first item reported about Amir, and second, because at his trial Amir vigorously denied that there was any previous assassination attempt.

The next day, *Maariv*'s headline read, "The Assassin Also Planned To Murder Peres." This was not only denied by Amir but was logistically imposssible even for Jesse James. So why the false leaks, reportedly, from the police interrogation?

Was There A Third Shamgar Murder Coverup?

Not everyone was terribly happy that Meir Shamgar was appointed to head the commission of inquiry into the assassination. Michal Goldberg of *Yediot Ahronot* reported; "The three judges cut short their afternoon session to hear the claims of former police officer Yitzhak Keren who was protesting outside the building. 'I demand that you step down,' Keren told Shamgar, 'It was during your tenure as the government legal adviser that you covered up the truth behind the murder of the soldier, Rachel Heller.'" Shamgar listened but did not react.

What Was Peres Trying To Say?

Shimon Peres' eulogy at Rabin's funeral contained a most intriguing passage. "Last Saturday," he said, "as we crossed arms, he told me that there was a high alert for an assassination attempt at this huge rally. We didn't know who would do it, nor did we expect the damage to be so great."

Peres seemed to have told the world that Rabin and he both knew about the coming assassination attempt at the rally but weren't told who would try it. Neither did they expect it to be fatal. Thirty days later, as many people pointed out to me, Peres, speaking at a memorial service to Rabin, said, "The bullets that pierced your chest did not cut down the fruits of your labor."

Ignoring the inappropriate metaphor, at that time the bullets were commonly known to have pierced his back.

What Was Eitan Haber's Role In All This?

As mystifying as Peres's eulogy was, nothing compares to Eitan Haber's for pure surrealism. For those who have forgotten the tiny details of this drama, Eitan Haber was Rabin's Director of the Prime Minister's Office. He went into Ichilov Hospital on the night of the murder and left with Rabin's bloody songsheet in hand. He announced the Prime Minister's death to the nation, then ran to Rabin's office and removed files from the cabinets. If that didn't appear suspicious enough, Haber increased the minions who suspected him of untold involvement by mounting a personal vendetta against the Amir family, appearing at every court session during Yigal Amir's trial and endlessly calling the Amirs a family of monsters. Without doubt, I receive more correspondence about the round, black hole in the song sheet than any other clue. No one can properly explain it but dozens of people have given it their best, if I may, shot.

One correspondent, Raanan Bavli sent me a copy of Haber's eulogy with the following comments: "This is getting interesting. I found a quote on the Internet from Chief Rabbi Lau who said that the song sheet was given to Leah Rabin at the hospital. However, no one but Peres has ever said the sheet had a hole in it. Also, the tapes show Rabin didn't even have his own sheet. He read from Raanan Cohen's sheet."

This is pretty typical of the intelligent, inquiring correspondence I receive. So, let us try and figure out what it is about this song sheet that ignites so much interest. First, a look at Haber's eulogy. He said, "Five minutes before you were shot, you sang from the sheet they gave you, so you could, as you always did, mouth the words. You had a thousand gifts and advantages but singing wasn't counted among them. You bluffed your way through the song and after, as always, you folded the sheet into four even sections and put it in your jacket pocket. At the hospital, they gave me the sheet, still folded into four even sections. I would like to read from the sheet, but it's difficult. Your blood covers the printed words. Your blood is on the Song Of Peace. This blood was drawn from you in your last moments of life to cover this sheet. Yitzhak, we miss you already."

It sounds like he misses the song sheet more. Almost his whole euology was about the sheet. As for Rabin, we learn he was fastidious about folding paper and couldn't sing very well. So what was the overwhelming interest Haber had in this piece of paper. Clues are given in his account which appeared in *Yediot Ahronot* on 11/6/95.

Haber was waiting for Rabin to show up at a party when word of the shooting reached him.

> "I jumped into the car and drove like a madman, arriving at the hospital within minutes. I ran toward the operating rooms. I didn't know where I was going or how to get there. On the way I saw his blood-soaked belongings and collected them."

Hospitals don't allow visitors anywhere near the operating rooms, yet Haber could just run, without knowing where he was going in a large hospital complex, into the operating area and see Rabin's blood-soaked belongings on the floor. Needless to say, Haber had no right to touch evidence, but he not only handled it, he collected it.

> "I knew something was wrong as soon as I entered the hospital and saw the driver, Menachem Damti. Someone said it was all over but our hopes rose when his blood pressure returned to 90. Leah Rabin arrived and I kept the bad news from her. Bye the bye, I made notes for the reporters and phoned the American Ambassador to inform the White House that Rabin was shot. Someone had to do it."

But why Haber, who was not a cabinet minister or even a Knesset member? Why would a lowly office director be the one to inform the White House of the shooting? This was in breech of diplomatic custom.

In all of Haber's account, there is not one mention of the song sheet. No one in the hospital gives it to him. As he tells it, he just picked it up off the floor and took it along with the other blood soaked belongings. Why didn't he turn them over to the police? Why was he holding onto this sheet at Rabin's funeral instead of it being held as state evidence in the police forensics laboratory? What other belongings did he take away before the police could get to them? Who authorized him to gather them up? What was he doing in the operating area in the first place? And all the while he was gathering Rabin's belongings, he still found the time to call the American ambassador and inform him Rabin was dying, as well as prepare a press statement. But he was too busy to tell Leah Rabin the truth.

The story was told, of a man on a mission.

Rabin with the song sheet minutes before shooting is heard.

The song sheet after the assassination.

RABIN MURDER
EYEWITNESS
COMES FORWARD

In late 1997, *Anashim* Magazine printed an interview with Mordi Yisrael which made me somewhat reluctant to include this chapter. He said he was sure he had convinced me that there was no conspiracy and he denied telling me that the gunshots sounded like "party poppers." That said, I insist that I accurately recorded his version of events and stand by what is written. Further, a London TV producer spoke to Mordi the day after I interviewed him and Mordi related the same story to him.

Despite some changes in his story, as *Anashim* noted, Mordi repeated almost verbatim the most important issues. He contradicted the Shamgar Comission findings by saying again that Rabin did not fall after the first shot, his bodyguard did not pounce on him, and Amir did not move closer to Rabin for the second and third shots. And this testimony is too important to be excluded despite far more minor alterations made later by Mordi.

Friday, September 26 was a banner day for the truth. *Yediot Ahronot's* weekend magazine chain published a four page exposé of the government coverup of Avishai Raviv's activities prior to the Rabin assassination.

The author of the article, Gadi Blum, wrote that the Attorney General, Edna Arbel, was deliberately hiding the findings of two government inquiries, led by Erin Shendar and Michael Eitan, into Raviv's role in the assassination.

Further, the article contended that Amir was being manipulated to stop the movement to arrest and question Raviv. That he demanded that his mother withdraw a petition to the Supreme Court to have Raviv investigated.

The article was very respectful towards me, calling me the "father of the Rabin conspiracy theory, which is given great credibility in Judea and Samaria." However, one quote was terribly wrong. I told Mr. Blum that I had been invited to a minister's office where his advisor informed me that the highest levels of the Likud secretly used the truth about the assassination against Labor in the previous election campaign. As Blum told it, I received my information from the minister himself. Despite the blunder, the article remains a most important stepping stone toward the final revelation of what really happened to Rabin the night he was murdered.

One person who read the article with great interest was Mordi Yisrael. He has become a permanent character in the assassination drama. He is the man on the Kempler film of the murder who Amir must circle to get a shot at Rabin. He stood just in front of Amir and was closest to Rabin when the shot was fired. Yet, up until now, he has been no more than a minor character in the play. That is about to change. What Mordi Yisrael has to say is utterly remarkable. A day after he read Blum's piece, he tracked me down and called me. We met the next morning.

I had already come to know him by face, having seen him hundreds of times on the Kempler film. Many times I heard rather sinister rumors about his alleged role in the murder. The rumors started as a result of an enormous blunder by the Shabak. When it released stills of the Kempler film to *Yediot Ahronot*, it superimposed another person over Amir's picture so sloppily that Amir is seen shooting with his left hand, though all witnesses saw him shoot with his right. Now, Amir's arm seems to have been resting on Mordi Yisrael's shoulder. Hence the whispered rumors that he was an accomplice. I never took such talk seriously, but I did take note that Mordi Yisrael was becoming an entrenched figure in the legend slowly being constructed around the Rabin murder.

Mordi is in his mid-twenties and lives with his parents in a fourth-floor apartment in Kiryat Gat. His father is a police investigator and objects to Mordi talking to me. "You are being interrogated again," he says. Mordi replies, "I'm just trying to figure out what happened. I have to know already." His mother is sympathetic.

On the evening of November 4, 1995, Mordi was on assignment for Tel Aviv College, where he was a media student. He was to tape as many politicians as he could for a mock radio report.

> "I had everything on tape. The machine was rolling right through the assassination. I was just behind Rabin, holding the mike and calling to him to offer a comment. In the cab on the way home I thought to myself that I recorded a historical event. But when I got home, nothing was on the tape. It was all fuzz. I've used the machine hundreds of times before and it always recorded. I couldn't understand why it didn't record at all. I would have noticed if the mike was pulled out."

Before delving into Mordi's recollection of the evening, it is advisable to review what the Shamgar Commission of Inquiry, and thus the government, tells us happened. The official version has Amir shooting Rabin in the back from 50 cm range. Immediately after, bodyguard Yoram Rubin fell on Rabin and covered him while both were prone on the ground. Amir was being held by two other bodyguards but managed to shoot, first Rubin and then Rabin from about 20 cm above them.

Here is what Mordi Yisrael, the eyewitness closest to the murder scene, says took place.

> "As I arrived backstage I asked a policeman if I could get past the barrier. He let me in without checking my person or tape recorder. At the time I thought this was really lax of him and later I thought it was this kind of laxness that caused the murder. Now I'm not so sure I wasn't deliberately allowed in. I say that because I was the only journalist around. There should have been lots of reporters questioning Rabin, but I was the only one. Just recently it began occurring to me that maybe there was a mix-up and I was let in because my description, short, young twenties, Sephardic, in short-sleeve shirt, matched Amir's.
>
> "As soon as I was in, I began interviewing the politicians roaming around the area. Then I saw Peres coming down the steps and decided to get him on tape. But he was acting very strangely. Instead of walking at a normal pace to his car, he darted straight at the crowd. I had to rush to keep up with him. Right then, I thought that something was wrong. Why was he in such a hurry and why did he expose himself to the crowd like that? He took no precautions when meeting the people yet he wasn't friendly to them either. He shook a few hands and left. I managed to ask him how he thought the rally went and he answered, 'Very successfully,' before he took off."

At this point, we watched the relevant section of the Kempler film. Mordi pointed himself out talking to Peres and I stressed that Peres then rushed straight to Rabin's car and stopped opposite it. While Peres was examining the vehicle with four Shabak agents, the film was cut. At the end of the cut Peres is seen talking with Rabin's driver Menachem Damti. Mordi was impressed. "Why was Peres in such a rush to look at Rabin's car?" he asked.

After succeeding in taping a perfunctory quote from Peres, Mordi saw Rabin descending the steps. He decided to capture him on tape as well. This would make his assignment a complete success. He approached the Prime Minister from behind and beseeched him to make a few remarks to his mike.

> "Even then I noticed how easy it was to get to Rabin. I saw his rear body-guard stop in his tracks to have a few words with a policeman. Rabin was totally uncovered and I just stepped up to him. He was ignoring my questions

and walking at a fast clip. Finally I got his attention and he turned around to answer me. Then I heard the shot. He turned to me simultaneously with the shot but I don't think either of us thought there was any danger because the noise wasn't like a gun shot, rather like a harmless party popper."

Mordi stopped the conversation, saying, "There's something in the film that bothers me." He fast-forwarded the video. What he had been saying answers one of the more nagging questions of the murder mystery: why did Rabin and only Rabin react to the shot by turning his head toward it? Until now I had answered that Rabin was the only one to feel the blast from the blank bullet and thus was the first to react. It wasn't a satisfying answer. That he was coincidentally turning to speak to Mordi made much more sense.

Mordi replayed the moment. "It didn't happen that fast," he said. "In the film Rabin turns his head in a split second. In reality, he turned to me at a perfectly normal speed."

Mordi had now verified one of the central claims of Rabin murder researcher Natan Gefen. Gefen insisted proof that the Kempler film was doctored existed in the speed that Rabin reacted to the first shot. Rabin turned his head around just .25 seconds after the shot was fired. The typical reaction speed of a man thirty years younger is .75 seconds. Said Gefen, "Rabin reacted three times faster to the shot than a much younger man typically would. And Rabin was not James Bond. He drank and wasn't fit. There is no way he would have reacted to the sound before any of his bodyguards."

Mordi reached the dramatic climax.

"Immediately after the shot, I heard someone shout from the direction of the crowd, 'They're blanks. They're blanks.' Just as Rabin and I made eye contact, Rabin's face suddenly displayed utter terror. He lifted his hands to eye-level, stared over my shoulder for a split second and then he hunched his shoulders and tried to run away. I turned around and saw Amir standing all by himself with his arm extended, pistol in hand. Then he shot twice in a row. I saw the blasts from both shots. But neither sounded like real gunshots; again, more like party poppers.

"Then I turned back and saw Rabin. It was pathetic. He was all alone, not a bodyguard near him, while Amir was hooting. He saw Amir but had nowhere to run. After the two shots were fired, his bodyguards finally jumped on him."

Mordi Yisrael testified to the Shamgar Commission but his testimony was completely ignored. You won't find Mordi Yisrael's name in the publicly released findings of the commission, though it might have turned up in the 30% of the report that was hidden from the public, supposedly for their own good. Mordi has never read either report and, like most Israelis, doesn't know what snake oil their politicians have been selling.

So I pulled out some files and showed them to Mordi for his reaction. First I showed him bodyguard Yoram Rubin's testimony to Shamgar: "I jumped on the Prime Minister, heard a shot and felt a jolt of electricity rush through my arm. Then I heard another shot...I waited for a hiatus in the shooting...and then said, "Yitzhak, can you hear me and only me, goddammit."

Mordi asked, "Is he saying he got shot on the ground and then Rabin?"

"Yes," I replied. "According to the official version, Rabin took the first shot from 50 cm while standing up, Rubin took the next shot from slightly under 50 cm while prone, and then Rabin took a similar shot."

"You mean Amir got closer for the last two shots?"

"Yes."

"Absolutely out of the question. There was a long gap between the first two shots, maybe three or four seconds. During that time Rabin ran away from Amir while he stood still. Rabin was a good two meters away from Amir when he was shot again. And, I repeat what I just said, Rabin was standing, not lying, all alone. Not Rubin nor anyone else was covering him, so Rubin could not possibly have been shot by Amir."

I show Mordi driver Menachem Damti's testimony to Shamgar which begins, "I heard the shot just as I was opening the door for Leah Rabin. The Prime Minister fell just half a meter from the car..."

"Leah Rabin," Mordi reacts, "was nowhere near the car. And Rabin fell a good two meters from the car. Damti is so mistaken it sounds like he's lying too."

Next I offer Mordi documents hidden from the public for his reaction: Chief Lieutenant Gladstein's findings that Rabin was shot point blank, Dr. Gutman's report that Rabin was shot through the chest and spine, Bernard Shechter's ballistics report that has Amir's gun shooting just once. I assure and reassure him that all the documents are real.

"These reports are describing another murder," he notes. "Rabin's spine couldn't have been shattered, he kept walking way from Amir. Amir never shot point blank; I saw the three gun blasts and I witnessed him taking two of his shots. He never got close to point blank range and the last two shots were from two meters away. If the ballistics report is accurate they had to have been examining another gun."

By now, Mordi was flummoxed. He was on the front line of the murder. He had a better view than anyone else. He was positioned to see the assassination from both the killer and the victim's point of view. Yet the Shangar

Commission told a story that had nothing to do with the truth as he saw it first hand. Worse for him, perhaps, were the police and medical reports which describe an entirely different murder, one in which Rabin is shot point blank and from the front. Yet surprisingly, Mordi would not accept the possibility of a conspiracy in the assassination.

The only solution, in my opinion, is the one now accepted widely. Amir shot blanks (party poppers), and Rabin was finished off in his car. Mordi will not believe this thesis. Yet he adds an eerie statement. "You know," he says, "There was a lot more I didn't tell you. Much stranger things. I'm not ready to tell them to anyone yet." We look at the Kempler film again. There is Mordi and there is Amir's gun. We see the blast and then watch Mordi flinch and duck.

"Instead of flinching," he asks, "what would have happened if I had grabbed Amir's arm and wrestled him to the ground?"

"My guess," I answered, "is you'd be well on the road to a successful political career by now."

23   THE CULPRITS
כג

The assassination of Yitzhak Rabin is a solvable crime. It begins not in Tel Aviv, but rather, in Hebron. There, in March 1994, another horrid crime was perpetrated. Twenty-nine Arabs were slaughtered in the Cave of the Patriarchs and a commission of inquiry was set up to get to the truth. It was led by the former chief justice of the Israeli Supreme Court, Meir Shamgar, who would later head the commission of inquiry into Rabin's death. And like the latter case, the Hebron commission was a blatant whitewash.

The very day of the massacre, an Arab reporter for the weekly news magazine *Yerushalaim* visited 25 survivors in six separate hospitals. There was no time for them to organize a conspiracy or coordinate their testimony. Further, some of the wounded were mere children. And one after another they reported that the man accused of the crime, Baruch Goldstein had at least one, perhaps two accomplices.

A dozen of these survivors testified to the Shamgar Commission that they saw an accomplice handing the shooter bullet clips as he ran out. And like the Rabin murder, strangely, nine of the soldiers who were supposed to guard the shrine were not on duty that morning. The three who were testified that they saw Goldstein enter followed a few minutes later by a civilian carrying a Galil assault weapon.

Shamgar ruled that Goldstein acted alone, that the soldiers who saw someone else follow him were mistaken and that all the Arab witnesses perjured themselves. The implication of his verdict was that Arabs lie and their testimony is worthless. No honest court in the world would have reached Shamgar's conclusion.

And, like his later commission into Rabin's murder, what was more significant was who didn't testify and what evidence wasn't admitted. First, no one knows to this day how Goldstein died. No autopsy was ordered and the circumstances of his demise remains unknown.

Second, and more important, was who didn't prevent the massacre. Goldstein knew the slaughter was coming and he told friends, including Shmuel Cytryn, later arrested without charge and imprisoned for months, that two days before the event he received notice from the army "to prepare for a massacre."

That should have been enough warning for a division of the General Security Services (Shabak), commonly called The Jewish Department, to go into preventive action. This most secret unit planted agents throughout the territories, supposedly to surveil radical Jews and restrict their activities. The massacre was a notable failure, yet the head of the unit, Carmi Gillon, was not called to testify at the Shamgar Commission. Perhaps this was because his brother, Ilan Gillon, was the registrar of the commission responsible for organizing testimony.

After the Shamgar whitewash, Gillon was named head of the Shabak, a strange reward in the aftermath of the Hebron fiasco. Or was the slaughter really a fiasco? What is known for certain is that the unit continued to incite and entrap those territorial Jewish residents who opposed the Rabin peace process. The most publicized case was that of the Kahalani brothers who received 12-year prison terms for attempted murder of Arabs. According to the Shabak they were caught in a sting operation in which the firing pin of their weapon was removed. They claim the weapon was planted in their vehicle. Either way, they were entrapped in a manner illegal in most democratic societies. (They were released from prison in February, 2000).

Of course, the unit's most famous agent was Avishai Raviv, whose duty was to provoke the murder of Yitzhak Rabin. He formed an organization called Eyal, which had no members but himself. He convinced a student on the campus of Bar Ilan University, Yigal Amir, to help him organize study groups in or near Hebron. Four teenage girls, students of Sarah Eliash, witnessed Raviv prodding Amir to kill Rabin in front of them, calling him a coward and a fake hero. This testimony was heard by the Shamgar Commission and was not included in the publicly released conclusions.

Raviv was no minor provocateur. It was he who had posters of Rabin dressed in a Gestapo uniform printed and distributed at a large rally, and it was he who organized a swearing-in ceremony broadcast on Israel television's Channel One a month and a half before Rabin's assassination. The so-called Eyal members vowed to kill anyone who betrayed the land of Israel. Later, participants in the performance testified that Raviv told them what to say, where to stand and the whole production was viewed as a put on. They did not realize they were setting up Amir as a patsy by creating a radical group for the public to identify him with.

Replacing Gillon as head of the anti-subversive unit was agent Kalo and he appointed agent Eli Barak as his deputy. To this day very little is publicly known about Kalo. But Barak is a different matter. The week after Rabin's murder, the wide circulation newspaper *Kol Ha'ir*, without naming him, accused him of being responsible for the assassination.

Much is known about Barak. He is a convicted drunk driver, wife swapper and stalker. After a near fatal accident caused by his intoxication, he lied to the police about who was driving the car. His friend and fellow wife swapper died in mysterious circumstances. And in the most publicized incident of all, he terrorized and stalked a radio reporter, Carmela Menashe. Instead of firing this security hazard, Rabin sent him abroad on a mysterious assignment and later approved his appointment in Hebron.

In the most obvious coverup of the Shamgar Commission, seven Shabak agents and officers involved in the "snafu" that led to Rabin's death, including Kalo, received notices that they were liable for criminal prosecution. Barak did not. Kalo was later exonerated by the commission despite being in charge of the Raviv operation but Barak, who was apparently Raviv's immediate superior, was not called to testify in open court.

A few persistent reporters tried tracking Barak down at his home in Kochav Yair but were rudely turned away by Shabak officers surrounding his block. The key to uncovering the truth clearly lies with Eli Barak but he has been protected, overly protected, by the government.

In February of 1996, the Jerusalem correspondent for *The London Observer*, Shay Bhatia, reported that he spoke with two Shabak agents fired since the assassination. They informed him that Amir was supposed to fire blanks and that Rabin's chief security aide Danny Yatom was involved in the preparations for the scam. His silence was bought by being appointed as chief of the Mossad, an incident eerily reminiscent of Carmi Gillon's rise to head of the Shabak after the Hebron massacre.

Of Gillon, it is well known that he was a far-leftist, who despised the settlers and was heard refering to them as "neo-Nazis." His attitude was revealed in his 1991 masters thesis completed at Haifa Unversity which analysed the settler movement from a perspective of hatred.

Two days before the assassination, despite pleas from subordinates not to leave the country before the rally in light of the national mood, Gillon flew to Paris. A joke that made the rounds after the assassination has Gillon calling Leah Rabin on the night of the murder and offering his deep condolences. She asks him what for. "Oops," he says, "I forgot about the time difference."

24
כד

AT LONG LAST: RABIN'S THIRD WOUND PROVEN

November 1998. It had been eighteen months since the last hidden documentation about the Rabin assassination had been uncovered. Since then some serious evidence had emerged about the political side of the murder. A year before, the government released some sections of the previously closed Shamgar Commission findings which incriminated Avishai Raviv far more deeply in widespread crimes of provocation. Two months later, one former Eyal activist, Benny Aharoni, signed a sworn statement to Knesset Member Michael Eitan that, under orders from Raviv, he phoned three dozen reporters and delivered the infamous "We Missed But We'll Get Rabin Next Time" message, well before the shooting was announced on the Israeli media. And journalist Adir Zik had gathered powerful evidence of Carmi Gillon's complicity in the murder.

But the tap had shut tight on any new medical, police or forensic documentation. It looked as though the evidence I had collected for this book would be the last of the proofs that Yigal Amir had not shot fatal bullets into Rabin. The strongest evidence was the testimony of Police Chief Lieutenant Baruch Gladstein proving that Rabin was shot point blank and Dr. Mordechai Gutman's surgeon's notes describing a frontal chest wound which passed through the lung before shattering the vertebrae at D5-6.

When this book was written, I had read Gutman's full surgical report, which included the description of three gunshot wounds and the publicly released procedural summation of November 5, which removed the frontal chest wound and shattered spine. Thus, it was Dr. Gutman's written word from the night of the murder versus his altered version of events, co-authored with Drs. Kluger and Hausner, the next day. Whenever Dr. Gutman was confronted with his report of the chest wound on the murder night, he answered that he had mistaken Rabin's ribs for his spine.

If so, that Dr. Gutman couldn't tell the difference between ribs and the spinal column, as one doctor attending a lecture of mine told the audience, he should be disbarred from ever practicing medicine again. However, another doctor did give Dr. Gutman the benefit of the doubt: if the bullet shattered the vertebrae at the point where the ribs join the spine, such a mixup was both logical and understandable.

The main problem was that we were missing reliable descriptions of Rabin's condition before and after the doctors went to work on him. Dr. Gutman's report of a frontal chest wound lacked overall perpective and seemed an oddity that could be sloughed off with the explanation that he was mistaken when he wrote it.

In early December, American filmmaker, Peter Goldman, arrived in Israel with the intention of gathering the evidence needed to justify raising funds for a full-length documentary based on my book. I gave him my contacts, who were new to him, but we shared one contact in common. I expressed the opinion that visiting him would be a waste of time. I had had a meeting with him a year and a half before and followed it up with two phone calls. It was all for naught; this contact had not provided me with any new evidence. Undaunted, Peter met him anyway and was well rewarded for following his instincts.

Just a few hours before departing the country, Peter presented me with three new documents. I immediately understood that they were the final pieces of the puzzle. We now had a complete diary of Rabin's treatment at Ichilov Hospital.

Document one was the initial visual diagnosis of Rabin by Dr. Gutman. Hastily written in English, the diagnosis reads, "GSW Abdomen and Chest": Gunshot wounds to the abdomen and chest.

When I read the word chest, I thought I had found the smoking gun. Rabin arrived with a chest wound. Amir never shot him in the chest. Case closed. I would have to change my book. There were only two wounds, not three. There was no third shot in the hospital. Rabin was shot in the chest in the car.

However, within a few days, two experts set me straight. A chest wound can also begin from the back if the bullet travels forward and injures the chest.

Page two was far more detailed. It begins with a description of Rabin's first bodily examination and provides us with indisputable proof of Rabin's condition immediately after he was placed on the examination table.

Page three was the summation of the operation. At last, we no longer had to depend on the public summation of November 5 to understand the cause of Rabin's death.

I now had the whole story in hand and it was told in the following reports:

1. First diagnosis
2. First bodily examination
3. Surgical procedure
4. Operation summation
5. Altered public summation

By the time I had completed my first version of this book, I had read reports 3 and 5. Four months after the book was released, I received reports 1, 2 and 4. And to my great relief, they confirmed my thesis conclusively. The documents, though not lengthy nor wordy, are surprisingly complicated and packed with information, which can be interpreted in different ways. Nonetheless, one piece of information cannot be disputed: *Rabin's first chest wound cannot possibly be the same one which Dr. Gutman described on the last page of his surgical procedure report.*

As recalled, Gutman operated on a wound beginning in the upper lobe of the right lung, which exited the lung in the direction of Dorsal Vertebrae 5-6, leaving a 2.5-3 cm exit wound in the lung before shattering the vertebrae. That is the wound Rabin ended up with.

Here is the wound he arrived with. According to the newly uncovered first bodily examination report, Rabin's chest wound was caused by, "an entrance wound in the area of the right shoulder blade which lodged under the skin in ICS3 at MCL 3-4."

> Translated: The bullet entered the right shoulder blade and took a straight line path to Intercostal Space 3 at Midclavicular line 3-4.

> Simplified: The bullet went from the right shoulder blade to just below the right nipple.

Dr. Gutman could not have mixed up the ribs and the spinal column because this bullet was lodged in the mid-section of the ribs, almost as far from the spine as is possible.

I received a detailed explanation from a physician who had the foresight to bring visual aids in the form of large scale skeletal charts. In report 3, Dr. Gutman does indeed begin the operation with procedures to treat a rear chest wound. And Rabin responds. His pulse returns to 130, his blood pressure to 90. Then without explanation as to why, his pulse drops to 60, his blood pressure also to 60 and then all vital signs disappear from the monitor. It is at this point that Dr. Gutman suddenly operates on a frontal chest wound which shatters the backbone.

The physician explained, "It's as if that wound came out of nowhere. The patient's vital organs had stopped functioning and other procedures were called for. There was no reason to begin a new operation, unless there was a new wound."

The physician then tried every hypothetical bullet path to match the frontal chest/spine wound Dr. Gutman finally operated on, with the rear chest wound Rabin arrived with, as described in reports 1 and 2. Even with the most deft of contortions, the wounds didn't match. In order for one bullet to do all the damage described in reports 1, 2, and 3, it would have to take the following journey:

Amir would have had to have shot Rabin in a near straight line from the side, not the back, something he did not do. The bullet would have entered the shoulder blade and carried on to the upper lobe of the right lung, switching directions to go down to Dorsal Vertebrae 5-6, which are in the mid-back. Then it would have had to have shattered the vertebrae and been deflected upward, entering and exiting the lung again before lodging just below the skin in the area of the right nipple.

The physician concluded, "If that was so, and I add that it most certainly wasn't so, why was the first diagnosis a straight line back to chest wound and why didn't Dr. Gutman report the two additional lung punctures? Even if somehow one bullet caused these two wounds, it was incumbent on the surgeon to accurately describe the damage."

Finally, all THREE of Rabin's wounds were revealed.

The first two wounds, to the chest and abdomen occurred before Rabin's arrival. The third, frontal chest wound, had to have been inflicted after he entered the hospital.

Of the second wound, the bullet entered the abdomen via the left flank. Dr. Gutman failed to notice another rather important detail as we shall soon see.

We now examine report 4, and what a tale it tells. The operation is now over and the surgical team writes its conclusion of their very busy night. And what a talented team it was. Department Heads all. No longer is Dr. Gutman the sole witness to the night's events. Though he writes the summation, it is witnessed by Drs. Kluger and Yekerevitch, anaethesiologist Dr. Ostrovski and nurses Evelyn and Svetlana. Svetlana, co-signs the report and adds signed confirmation, finally, of Dr. Gutman's surgical procedures.

Let's begin easy. At the bottom of the page are the times of the whole night's events. Rabin was received at 22 hours, on the table at 22:05, under anaesthesia at 22:10, operated on beginning at 22:15 and ending at 23:30.

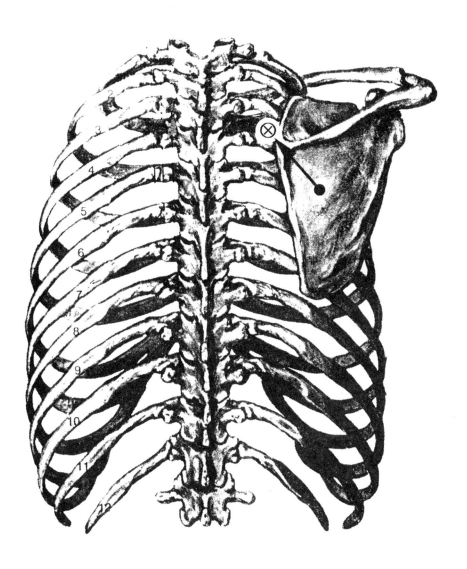

The initial "chest wound" documented on the first bodily examination report at Ichilov. The bullet entered near the right shoulder blade and travelled almost straight through to just below the right nipple.

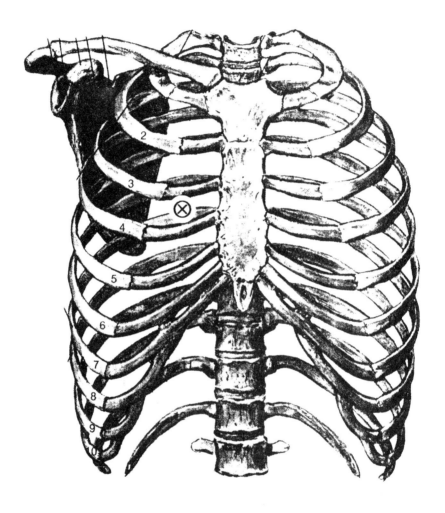

Front view Bullet entrance point for Rabin's third wound: the frontal chest wound. The bullet entered between ribs 3-4, traveled downwards through the right lung, and shattered Dorsal Vertebrae 5-6 upon exit.

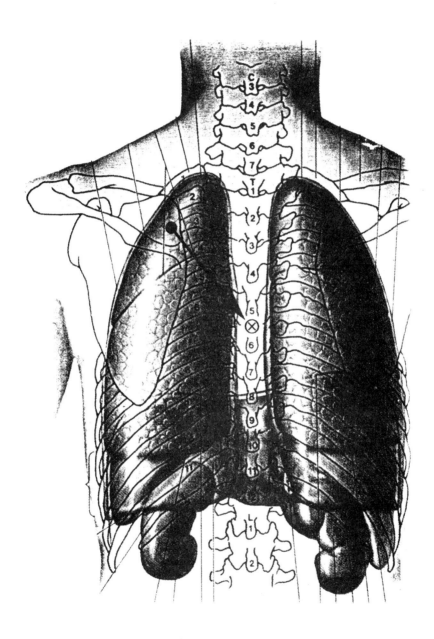

Rear view Exit point at Dorsal Vertebrae 5-6. Note that Amir, shooting from behind, could not have been responsible for this wound.

The problem here is that Rabin's death was officially announced at 23:20. We'll assume for now that the clock was wrong in the operating theater.

The real story is at the top of the page. First, it goes a long way toward confirming the laboratory conclusions of Chief Lieutenant Gladstein by noting that Rabin was shot from close range. Next, in report 1, we read that Rabin was admitted with gunshot wounds to the chest and abdomen. By report 4, some new wounds seem to have been added. The major wounds are still Gun Shot Wounds to chest and abdomen. But now four secondary wounds are added in English. They are:

- GSW to right lung

- Laceration of spleen

- Hemorrhagic shock

- Spinal shock?!

Dr. Gutman added the question and exclamation marks for emphasis, apparently indicating that this was the final cause of death. At least, that's what the physician and an IDF officer from the medical corps both guessed. Laceration of the spleen and hemoragic shock were likely internal wounds caused by the shot to the flank.

However, the first and last wounds are highly problematic, as the physician explains. "First, you must accept that, unlike the nearly conclusive evidence of two chest wounds that we examined before, this document is open to much more interpretation. Still, some really bothersome questions should be asked.

"Let's look at the secondary gunshot wound to the lung. Why would the doctors have even mentioned it? They reported a major gunshot wound to the chest and that, except in the rarest of injuries, includes the lung. What's the point of mentioning the lung wound again unless it came from another gunshot?"

The Shamgar Commission examined these very same documents and asked the same question. They were told that the second wound to the right lung was caused by the bullet that entered the flank. It passed through the spleen and stomach before lodging in the right lung. That is the official version held by the Israeli government and accepted by the judges at Yigal Amir's trial.

However the physician notes a fact the Shamgar Commission somehow missed. In order for a bullet shot in the left flank to reach the right lung, it has to pass through the left lung and most likely the heart. If the doctors were so fastidious about noting a secondary wound to the right lung, why didn't they record the entry and exit wounds that must have occurred in the left lung?"

And now the biggest issue of all, spinal shock. Recall that the state pathologist Dr. Yehuda Hiss conducted a limited autopsy on Rabin after Dr. Gutman's team had completed its work and found no damage to the spinal column. Recall also, that based on this conclusion, the Shamgar Commission and the judges at Yigal Amir's trial concluded that Rabin suffered no spinal damage. And finally, recall that the film of the assassination shows Rabin walking after the shot to his back, an impossibility if vertebrae 5 and 6 were shattered as Dr. Gutman reported.

Well, now it's not only Dr. Gutman reporting spinal shock. It's also five other members of his team. We should put them all in a courtroom and ask each why they agreed to appear on a report which concluded that Rabin died of spinal shock when the government of Israel's Justice Ministry and courts insist contrary.

I asked the physician, can spinal shock be caused by something other than breakage in the vertebrae or spinal cord? Perhaps a severe bruise or shaking can cause spinal shock. "Out of the question," he replied. "Spinal shock is the trauma resulting from a break or breaks in the spinal column. The breaks can be in the outer vertebrae or in the cord, but there is no other definition of spinal shock."

The physician made another poignant observation. "When the patient arrived, the doctors did not record any symptoms of spinal shock. Again this is possible but hard to understand. One of the first things doctors look for in shooting cases is spinal shock. It's very easy to diagnose. When the spinal nerves are severed, the blood stops pumping naturally and is forced downward by gravity. So, typically, the upper body is white and the lower body, red. The victim was shot at 9:45 and examined at 10:05. You would expect that twenty minutes after being shot in the spine, spinal shock would be detected and diagnosed."

The physician was reluctant to let me hear what I was waiting all these long months to prove. He would not say that the summation proved there was a third shot at Rabin from the time he was admitted to Ichilov Hospital but he stated,

> "If I didn't know who the victim was or the circumstances of his death, I think I'd have to conclude that the patient received another wound subsequent to his initial admission. But I would advise you to stress your strongest points and they are that two separate chest wounds are reported

by Dr. Gutman and that it is inconceivable that Rabin had no spinal damage. The six members of the operating team were too skilled to have all been wrong about that."

There you have it. It is a certainty that Rabin suffered a frontal chest wound and spinal shock, neither of which Yigal Amir could physically have caused. But there is even more to the documents than just the description of the wounds. There is confirmation of a vital vignette in my book.

I recounted an episode told to me by Zeev Barcella, editor of the country's largest circulation Russian-language newspaper, *Vesti*. On the morning of the assassination, he received a phone call from a Russian-born operating nurse who told him, "The media is lying about Rabin's wounds. I saw them. His spinal cord was shattered and they're saying it wasn't." Ninety minutes later the nurse called Barcella back and with well-remembered fear in her voice said, "I didn't call you before and you don't know who I am." Then she hung up the phone.

The newly uncovered documents revealed new names to me of people who were in the operating theater that night. The nurse's first name, Svetlana, and her signature were on the surgical summation. By comparing another document I possessed, I discovered her full name, Svetlana Shlimovitz. I found her phone number, introduced myself as best I could and had the following short conversation:

"Svetlana, I would like to know what happened to Rabin in the operating theater."

"How did you get my name?"

"You signed the surgical summation report."

"I don't work there anymore and I can never say what happened. Bye." And she hung up.

Barcella's story was true as well. As was my book. I got it right the first time around.

25
כה

CONCLUSION

Yitzhak Rabin's Memorial Day in 1999 was indeed memorable because of the remarkable events which preceded it. A week before, MK Ophir Pines abused his political rights and pressured the Steimatzky book chain from selling this book openly on its shelves. Frankly, I could not have been more delighted. There is nothing so healthy for a book as being banned. The Israeli media including *Maariv, Haaretz, The Jerusalem Post* and *Vesti* rushed to my defense. Leah Rabin told viewers of *Erev Chadash* that Pines was wrong and people should be permitted to read my book. Steimatzky received hundreds of complaints from irate customers and returned the book to its shelves. And this book made the national bestseller lists in Israel.

A few days later, Nissim Mishal announced that he would present a document on his television program, proving the Rabin assassination could have been prevented. Minutes before he was to go public with the evidence, State Attorney-General Elyakim Rubinstein banned him from doing so. The next day, Rubinstein placed a nationwide gag order on the document. Like the Ophir Pines book banning, Rubinstein's panicked reaction boomeranged and the whole country discussed what the government could be hiding.

Once the document appeared on the Internet, the public realized why Rubinstein had taken his drastic measures. What he tried to hide from the public were the protocols of a 1996 meeting at the office of Attorney-General Michael Ben Yair. The participants included the heads of the Shabak's Jewish Department, Eli Barak and Hezi Kalo and State Prosecutor, Edna Arbel. Their task was to pressure Ben Yair to close planned indictments against Avishai Raviv and Eitan Oren for staging the notorious Eyal swearing-in ceremony on Har Herzl.

Not only did the public receive conclusive proof of collusion between the Shabak and the Judiciary to protect Raviv and Oren, but it was also informed that the previous State Prosecutor, Dorit Beinish, had deliberately incriminated an innocent Bar Ilan University student in order to protect Raviv's cover.

If that wasn't shocking enough, the next day Dahlia Pelosoff-Rabin's interview in *Olam Ha'isha* was published and, what do you know...she revealed that she didn't believe the official version of her father's murder. There were too many unanswered questions, she insisted, which demanded a new commission of inquiry to answer them. On the evening of the memorial ceremony, her brother Yuval Rabin joined in, telling Channel Two News, "If there isn't a new commission of inquiry, there will be many more Chamishes in the future." I was touched.

And lo and behold, the public finally woke up. According to a Gallup poll conducted for Channel One, 57% of Israelis were in favor of opening a new commission of inquiry into the Rabin assassination, while only 18% were opposed. *The Jerusalem Post* poll found 65% in favor of reinvestigating the assassination.

My work and that of my colleagues had not been in vain.

And now I present the latest evidence for the newest edition of the book. Let us begin with two medical documents recently discovered.

In late 1999, two Israel-based TV producers were in America negotiating with a major network for a full length documentary film based on this book. The network executives were adamant that we track down a vital document: the complete State Pathologist's report written by Dr. Yehuda Hiss. They insisted that, without a comparison of the official pathologist's findings, on which the Shamgar Commission of Inquiry had based its findings, the contradictions in the police and hospital reports were of greatly reduced value. One of the producers called me in great agitation and nearly demanded that I track down a copy and in a hurry.

Until now I had utilized sections of the pathologist report reprinted by the newspaper *Hatzofe* in 1997. I suggested that the producer contact the reporter of the article, Hagai Huberman. She did and he said he had misplaced the material. Next, the producer called Yigal Amir's lawyer, Shmuel Fleishman, who informed her, "I have the report in my safe but it is untouchable. I can let you see everything else but I'm forbidden by law to open that report to you." Finally, the producer called the State Pathologist's Office at the Legal Medicine Department of the Sackler Faculty of Medicine. The office manager was aghast at her request and told the producer that she'd have to go to court to try and get it.

After two weeks the task looked hopeless. Yet how nice it is to have good contacts. Natan Gefen, who has recently published his own book on the Rabin assassination called *The Fatal Sting*, and my Russian-language editor, Dr. Michael Bronstein, acquired the report for me.

After over three and a half years, I had the full State Pathologist's Report on Yitzhak Rabin in my hands...And what a tale it tells. What a simply incredible fable most of it is, yet powerful truth remains within its blatant obfuscations.

Dr. Hiss's pathological examination of Yitzhak Rabin began at approximately 2 AM, November 5, or two and a half hours after Rabin was pronounced dead on the operating table. The prelude to the report is a declaration by Dr. Hiss that what he writes is legally binding, as if he had sworn an oath in court.

Let us begin. I will present statements from the report and offer some explanations of their significance.

1. The Other Pathologist

Prelude: "Assisting me was Eli Lipshtein."

Significance: On July 6, 1996, the Supreme Court of Israel heard a petition based on the testimony of a taxi driver, who drove an unnamed pathologist to Ichilov Hospital. The passenger produced his hospital identification card and told the driver that he was a pathologist, who examined Rabin. He claimed Rabin was shot three times, not twice as the government was saying, and that there was something in Rabin's clothes that could give the truth away. Until now, it was assumed that Dr. Hiss had to be the passenger, despite legitimate doubts, because he was the only pathologist named by the Shamgar Commission. Now we may have identified the real pathologist whose information became the basis for a Supreme Court petition.

> Section One, Clause Five: "In the upper left third of the back...skin was missing in a round shape with a diameter of 7 cm...There was no gunpowder nor powder burns around the wound...In a detailed examination we found the path of the wound to be from back to front...passing through ribs 5 and 6, with a break in rib 6."

Significance: Dr. Hiss is describing the first shot to the back, which Chief Lieutenant Baruch Gladstein of the Fibers and Polymers Laboratory of Israel Police determined to be from just under 20 cm range. This range would explain the lack of gunpowder and powder burns.

Nothing, however, can explain his total misreading of the wound. Dr. Mordechai Gutman, in his surgeon's notes, three other doctors, and two nurses in the operation summary all agreed that a bullet entered D5-6, that is Dorsal Vertebrae 5 and 6, shattering the vertebrae. They make no mention ever of ribs 5 and 6. Dr. Hiss has altered the testimony of the surgical team which operated on Rabin, changing vertebrae to ribs.

> *Section One, Part B, paragraph one: "At the bottom of the left side of the back above the waist...there is missing skin with the dimensions of .8x1.4 cm...In the surrounding skin there is no sign of powder wounds or gunpowder..."*

Significance: Chief Lieutenant Gladstein testified at Yigal Amir's trial that, because of the massed concentrations of gunpowder and other materials in this shot, he determined it to be from point blank range. And the tiny hole described by Dr. Hiss confirms the range. So where did the powder go? Perhaps it stayed on the clothing which protected it from the skin?

> *Section Two, Part A, paragraph two: (Dr. Hiss is now examining Rabin's clothing) "On the fringes of the underwear was a tear whose dimensions were .2x6 cm...Surrounding the tear were no signs of powder burns or gunpowder..."*

Significance: Chief Lieutenant Gladstein described the 6 cm tear and explained that only a point blank shot could cause the tear. When the barrel of a gun is on the skin, he testified, the gases in the cartridge have nowhere to escape. This causes an explosion on the skin, which tears the clothing. And Chief Lieutenant Gladstein testified that the tear in Rabin's clothing contained concentrated amounts of gunpowder and other materials.

So why didn't Dr. Hiss find them? Or more likely, why did he make them disappear? Could it be because Yigal Amir never shot from anywhere near point blank range and the evidence had to be made to fit that fact?

One of the Greatest Breakthroughs in the Rabin Murder Investigation

> *Section Two, Part B, Paragraph three: (Dr. Hiss is examining Rabin's shirt) "In the front of the shirt, on the left side, in the lower third, is a round hole with a diameter of .6 cm."*

> *Section Two, Part C, paragraph 3: (Dr. Hiss is examining Rabin's undershirt) - "In regards to the hole in the front of the undershirt, we could not find any possible tear in the fabric to account for it."*

Significance: The official government version has Rabin shot twice in the back. And that's it. There is not supposed to be any frontal wound. At the heart of my argument that Yigal Amir did not shoot the fatal bullets at Rabin is the fact that literally every doctor and nurse who treated Rabin or entered the operating theater reported a third frontal wound. But Yigal Amir, according to all witnesses and the film of the assassination, never, ever shot from the front or had a chance to do so. So that wound was made to disappear from the official records of Rabin's murder.

And now we have the official pathology report on Rabin, written by the State Pathologist, reporting that Rabin's shirt and undershirt had a bullet-sized hole in the front.

No wonder this report is banned. It shatters the government's version to pieces. I sat with two veteran journalists and one academic. We tried to make sense of it all. Why would Dr. Hiss so clearly cover up Rabin's wounds throughout his report, yet report the most damning fact of all: that he was shot from the front?

The academic observed that this report had to have been censored and undergone different drafts, quite likely under the watchful eyes of some panicked Shabak officers. As with the assassination film, the Shabak censors just didn't have the expertise to clean the report of all the truth. The journalist reached a different conclusion: *Most likely the shirt was shot after Rabin was dead to try and match the very real hole in the front of his chest.*

Dr. Joshua Backon conducted extensive research into the significance of this report and concluded:

"All the forensic evidence proves that only an entrance wound can create a round hole. Exit wounds are jagged and uneven. Hiss is reporting a frontal gunshot."

Other Recent New Developments

The Gilion Nituah

I was convinced that the Pathologist's Report was going to be the last medical document recovered. Then on December 30, 1999, Dr. Bronstein faxed me the Gilion Nituah, written by Dr. Mordechai Gutman about half an hour after he completed his by-now-famous Surgeon's Notes, which reported the frontal chest wound, which continued to the backbone shattering vertebrae D5-6.

A little background. There has been a widespread attempt to negate the significance of Dr. Gutman's notes by writing them off as erroneous. For instance, Tom Segev wrote in *Haaretz*, "Chamish, admittedly, does present a most peculiar document from a surgeon who reports a frontal chest wound to Rabin. The most common conclusion is that the doctor was mistaken." Segev does not bother to mention that another eight doctors and nurses reported the same wound.

Most surprising to me has been the effort of Dr. David Chen to dismiss the significance of the frontal wound. He asked me,

> "Why stress that wound when you have all the proof you need in the lower back wound? Shamgar concluded that Amir shot downward from above Rabin. Yet this bullet moves horizontally from the waist, to the spleen, to the diaphram, to the lung. No bullet shot downward can take a 90 degree turn sideways. That's all the proof you need that Amir couldn't have shot fatal bullets at Rabin. There's no need to confuse the public with a frontal chest wound.
>
> "I've spoken with Rabin's surgeons. They tell me that Dr. Gutman made a mistake when he wrote that the bullet exited the lung towards the spine. He meant to write that the bullet entered the lung. He was flustered, that's all. You can understand that, can't you?"

I could have until I received the Gilion Nituach. This document was written well after the operation, when Dr. Gutman could have been sipping coffee beside his desk. And he reports on the second page of the Gilion:

> "The tear in the lung leads to D5-6-7, crushing and shattering the backbone."

Not only does Dr. Gutman confirm his original notes, he adds another shattered vertebra at D7. He might have been mistaken once, but there is no chance he made the same mistake twice.

Dr. Gutman's Headaches

One of the most intrepid truthseekers has been Asher Zuckerman, editor of the religious newspaper *Kol Hashavuah*. In November, 1999, he broke the disturbing report on the condition of the head of the surgical team which operated on Rabin, Dr. Mordechai Gutman.

For the previous five weeks Dr. Gutman had been incarcerated in Tel Hashomer Hospital with headaches that had all but incapacitated him. His doctors have sent his test results to hospitals around the world and could not find the cause of his debilitating affliction.

Matching Serial Numbers

At a recent lecture, a member of the audience asked to speak with me privately, requesting that I do not reveal his name. He opened the Hebrew version of this book to the page where I presented the report on Hagai Amir's weapons from the police ballistics laboratory. Hagai Amir was imprisoned for keeping an arsenal of weapons in his home and for giving his brother Yigal the bullets which supposedly murdered Rabin. Included in the armory was a pistol whose serial number was noted.

The audience member took out his own weapon and asked me to read the serial number. It was the very same number as Hagai Amir's pistol. How could that be, I asked? He explained, "The night after the murder, the Shabak raided my house and took my gun and bullets. They had to have handed them over to the police, claiming they actually belonged to Hagai Amir. Then they were returned to me."

The Blood-stained Songsheet

Remember Rabin's blood-soaked song sheet held by Eitan Haber at his funeral? The week after the murder, a local Ashdod newspaper interviewed a hospital worker who insisted that he saw the songsheet fall out of Rabin's jacket pocket and that there was no blood on it. The implication is that after Haber absconded with the sheet from Ichilov, the blood was deliberately stained on the paper.

More recently, in 2000, two TV teams working on the story of Rabin's murder managed to film the songsheet in the Prime Minister's Archives in Jerusalem. Remember the round black stain the size of a bullet in the songsheet held at Rabin's funeral by his speechwriter Eitan Haber? Well it's gone. It is no longer on the song sheet the government is saving in its archives.

Avishai Raviv's Trial

Finally, after several postponments, Avishai Raviv went on trial in Jerusalem in February 2000. But the court was closed to the public and the press. The trial ended, with virtually no information available to the public as to what had transpired. Recently, I spent two hours in the office of Raviv's lawyer, Eyal Shomroni-Cohen, and I received an explanation as to why the court ordered the trial closed to the public. Raviv, who was charged with not preventing Rabin's murder, went after the truth, my way, because he was innocent of the charge against him. He did not know about Rabin's impending murder, only about a fake assassination attempt. Raviv's lawyer asked the court to supply him with Rabin's clothing, to check the range of the shots, his x-rays to determine how many times he was shot, and the song sheet, to test whether Rabin's blood is on it.

Why Was There No Ambulance on the Scene?

In a profound piece of detective work, Dr. David Chen discovered the identities of one doctor and two paramedics who sat in an ambulance not twelve feet away from where Rabin was shot by Amir's blank bullets. After the first shot was heard, they ran towards Rabin and were physically prevented from reaching him by Rabin's bodyguards. The doctor was actually forced to the ground.

An Update on the Kahalani Brothers

On December 6, 1999, I appeared in a discussion group with Knesset members Michael Eitan, Nomi Blumental and Gideon Ezra, former Shabak Deputy Chief. Ezra was challenged by attorney Mordechai Mintzer to explain the twelve year sentence of the Kahalani brothers. He replied that they were dangerous terrorists who were planning to mass murder Arabs. I said to him, "I have a report from the police ballistics laboratory from the night before the weapons were discovered in the Kahalani brothers' possession. The police had the rifles and, therefore, planted them the next day, not in their car but in a vehicle owned by a Shabak agent named Yves Tibi. The Kahalani brothers were set up and I can prove it." Ezra answered, "That's clear," and then stopped himself. Draw your own conclusions. The audience of 300 had no trouble doing so.

In February 2000, the brothers were secretly released from prison, seven years early, for "good behavior." Again my claims were proven correct and, as usual, no one thanked me.

The French Connection?

In my previous edition's epilogue, I presented numerous theories that had been published elsewhere about possible international connections. One was that Henry Kissinger had a hand in the murder. I did not support the theory, I merely offered it as an indication of how other investigators were thinking.

If an international connection exists, and I am certain it does, the trail leads to France. In December 1995, a French journalist, Pierre Lurcat, reminded readers in his Jewish student paper, that President Mitterand had once faked his own assassination in a scandal, called the Observatoire Affair, that haunted him his whole career. The sympathy which arose from the phony murder attempt vaulted Mitterand's career to the top. Lurcat claimed Peres and Mitterand discussed how to do the same thing for Rabin to save his failing peace process with the PLO. Pierre told me, "I was only using my logic, I had no solid evidence. Then the authorities came down so hard on me and the newspaper that I surmised I got it right. I was a law student at the time, I'm an attorney now, and the French media turned me into a lunatic."

Then I was reminded that Peres' ally, the secretive French media mogul, Jean Frydman financed the rally where Rabin was murdered. And that Shabak chief Carmi Gillon spent the night of the assassination in Paris.

We all knew that. However, a correspondent sent me a rather chilling newspaper quote. Not long after the assassination, Gillon was asked why he was in Paris on that night and he explained that he was visiting Yaacov Perry in the hospital. Could it really be that the current and previous Shabak chiefs were both in France on the fatal night? So far, there has been no confirmation. Since then Gillon has refused to explain his decision to fly to Paris on November 3, 1995.

But there is no denying the bizarre incident in early 1996 when Jacques Chirac went crazy in the Old City of Jerusalem. Peres had sent Yoram Rubin to guard Chirac. His French bodyguards informed him who Rubin was and Chirac ran to the nearest reporters nearly crying that he did not need Israeli bodyguards. That he'd feel safer with Arab guards protecting him. There are pictures of Rubin behind Chirac to prove this incident.

Rabin's Last Days

Twelve days before the murder, the Abu Dis Agreement, which divided the city of Jerusalem into two, was signed in Paris. Rabin was never informed that the agreement was signed because he would not have approved it.

I have traced nearly every moment of the last month of Rabin's life and there is no doubt about it; he spent his last days trying to get Israel out of the peace process he was forced to initiate.

Take just three days as examples. On October 20, Rabin was in New York for the United Nations' 50th anniversary celebrations. While there, as reported in Haaretz, Warren Christopher and Dennis Ross tried to trick him into meeting Syrian Foreign Minister Shara and agreeing to an Israeli pullback to the shores of the Kinneret. Rabin let loose a loud, vindictive attack against the American deceit and declared that he was pulling out of the peace process.

The next day, October 21, he gave his answer to the Golan withdrawal demands. From the podium of the UN he declared that he came from Jerusalem, the eternally undivided capital of Israel and that the problems of the Middle East were not caused by Israeli stubbornness but by Arab terror.

The next day, on Otober 22, he flew to Washington and with AIPAC's help, oversaw the passage of two congressional laws. The first stated that American aid to the PLO would cease if it declared a state; the second declared that Jerusalem would never be divided.

Rabin was rebelling against the most powerful men on earth and he knew the risk. Rabin died a hero.

A Final Bombshell

I save the biggest surprise for last. My original thesis was that the person, who closed the door to Rabin's limousine—the fourth person in the car—must have been the murderer. I cannot stand by that thesis for certain anymore. There is a high degree of certainty that the fourth person has been identified.

In the Spring of 1998, I received a videotape from England. It was made on the evening of Rabin's funeral. It is a recording of a Channel Four (Britain) talk show. The guests include the Jewish scholar Dr. Hugo Green, the editor of the *Jewish Chronicle*, Ned Temko, and a pretty Israeli girl in her late teens or early twenties, Yifah Barak, a student at Middlesex University in London.

The moderator asked Barak how she first heard of the murder. "I was sitting at home when I got a phone call from Israel. My mom said, "He was murdered." I asked who was murdered and she said, "Rabin was murdered. Everyone was crying. It was a terrible situation."

The moderator asked, "You knew people close to the murder, didn't you?"

"Yes," Barak replied. "A friend of my sister's was in the car he was driving in and he actually fell on her after he was shot. She's in hospital now for shock."

After viewing this amazing interview, I phoned a journalist friend in London and asked him to track down Yifah Barak. He went to Middlesex University and found her address in the student records. He went to her flat and she told him her sister's friend, who was in Rabin's car, was the driver Menachem Damti's twelve year old daughter.

For a year, I sat on this information until I could find some confirmation of its veracity. To this day, I have not been able to find out who Yifah Barak is, nor how her family received such sensitive information. In the summer of 1999, television producer Jay Bushinsky sent a crew to London to interview Barak. She confirmed that Damti's daughter was the fourth person in the car and added details, such as this girl, now 17 years old, lives a life of personal terror, constantly sleeping in different locations.

What was she doing in the car in the first place? Jay Bushinsky's explanation was that she was waiting for her father to give her a ride home. He believes that she was well known to the bodyguards and would not have aroused suspicion by sitting in the limousine. In short, she was there by accident. And accidentally, she witnessed Rabin's murder. And that is why the driver, her father, took nine minutes to arrive at Ichilov. A hysterical teenaged girl had to be removed from the car before he could carry on to the hospital.

Subsequently, in May, 1999, two TV teams, one from the Tel Aviv University Communications Department, the other from the highly respected MGI Productions, were hard at work sorting out the Rabin murder. They teamed up to interview two highly nervous people, Rabin's driver Menachem Damti and his 22 year old daughter, Reut.

Damti acknowledged that one of his daughters, Reut, was beside Rabin's car and, indeed, she appears in the assassination film standing beside her father. After all this time, Damti acknowledged that his daughter was at the murder scene, but the film proved she wasn't in the car.

Finally, Reut Damti agreed to be interviewed and added to her father's claim that she couldn't have been in the car because she was outside. She was then shown Yifah Barak's interview and admitted that a lot of people did call her house on the murder night to see if everyone was alright. She added that there was nothing strange about her being in the sterile area, her two uncles were there, too.

Damti had invited his family to witness the grand fake assassination in which he would play a starring role. One of his invited guests was likely his OTHER, twelve year old, daughter.

Yifah Barak was phoned in London to get her side of things. She stood by her story but added vital details. She never claimed Reut Damti was in the car. Reut was her own age. It was her younger sister, Karen Barak, who called the Damti home to inquire about the other daughter, who was twelve at the time. And that is who, most likely, was an accidental witness to the Rabin assassination.

Next, Dr. Michael Bronstein called with remarkable information. He found a section of the Shamgar Report detailing Damti's actions on the murder night. Incredibly, after dropping Rabin off at the rally, he drove away, picked up his family and returned two daughters and at least one brother to the sterile area.

If this version of events is the correct one, in other words, if this girl was not in the car for sinister purposes, what are we left with? We have proven beyond dispute that Rabin was alive and well when he was pushed into the limousine. But he arrived at Ichilov Hospital with two bullets in his back, one shot from point blank range. So he had to have been shot twice in the car.

The passengers were the bodyguard, Yoram Rubin; the driver, Menachem Damti and his daughter; the policeman, Pinchas Terem; and Rabin himself. Menachem Damti could not have driven the car and shot point blank, his daughter appears to have been an accidental witness, presumably Terem got into the car after Rabin was shot, and Rabin did not shoot himself in the back twice...